PLACES OF PROMISE

Also by Cynthia Woolever and Deborah Bruce
From Westminster John Knox Press

A Field Guide to U.S. Congregations: Who's Going Where and Why
Beyond the Ordinary: Ten Strengths of U.S. Congregations

PLACES OF PROMISE

Finding Strength in Your Congregation's Location

Cynthia Woolever and Deborah Bruce

Westminster John Knox Press
LOUISVILLE • LONDON

Book design by PerfecType, Nashville, Tennessee
Cartoons: © *Dennis McKinsey*
Cover design: Mark Abrams
Cover photography courtesy of Getty Images, Alamy, and Joey Harrison

First edition
Published by Westminster John Knox Press
Louisville, Kentucky

This book is printed on acid-free paper that meets the American National Standards Institute Z39.48 standard. ∞

PRINTED IN THE UNITED STATES OF AMERICA

08 09 10 11 12 13 14 15 16 17 — 10 9 8 7 6 5 4 3 2 1

Library of Congress Cataloging-in-Publication Data

Woolever, Cynthia.
    Places of promise : finding strength in your congregation's location / Cynthia Woolever and Deborah Bruce. — 1st ed.
        p. cm.
        ISBN 978-0-664-23023-4 (alk. paper)
    1. Parishes—United States. 2. Demography—United States. 3. Christian leadership—United States. 4. Pastoral theology—United States. I. Bruce, Deborah. II. Title.

    BV700.W67 2008
    250.973—dc22

                                                                2007034276

CONTENTS

Thanks

ACKNOWLEDGMENTS

WE GIVE SPECIAL THANKS . . .

To Ida Smith-Williams, Research Services, who managed the multiple databases from the project's very beginning. This project wouldn't have happened without her tenaciousness, good memory, and sense of humor.

To Zubeyir Niscanci, Hartford Institute for Religion Research, for his management and analysis of the contextual data. This book wouldn't have happened without his careful and thoughtful contributions.

To colleagues in Research Services, Presbyterian Church (U.S.A.): Keith Wulff (coordinator), Charlene Briggs, Perry Chang, John Marcum, Jamie McCulloch, David Prince, and Christy Riggs.

To colleagues in the Hartford Institute for Religion Research and Hartford Seminary, particularly: David Roozen (director), Carl Dudley, Adair Lummis, James Nieman, Mary Jane Ross, Scott Thumma, and Sheryl Wiggins.

To colleagues who served as consultants: Ann Deibert, Robert Dixon, Trey Hammond, and Herb Miller.

To Tony Healy of Visions-Decisions, who provided U.S. Census data for participating congregations.

To colleagues who directed the Leader study: Jackson Carroll and Becky McMillan, the Pulpit & Pew Project of the Ormond Center, Duke University.

To other colleagues whose comments and work added much: Dale Jones, of the

Church of the Nazarene and Association of Statisticians of American Religious Bodies; Philip Barlow, of Hanover College; and Mark Silk, of Trinity College.

To research colleagues who directed the denominational oversamples: Roger Dudley, Bryan Froehle, Mary Gautier, Kirk Hadaway, Richard Houseal, Phil Jones, Matthew Price, Marty Smith, and Craig This.

To international colleagues with whom we collaborated on the International Congregational Life Survey and whose earlier work set the stage for this project: project initiators, Peter Kaldor and Dean Drayton; Phillip Escott, Alison Gelder, and Roger Whitehead (England); Norman Brookes (New Zealand); and John Bellamy, Keith Castle, Howard Dillon, Robert Dixon, Ruth Powell, Tina Rendell, and Sam Sterling (Australia).

To our funding organizations and their officers: Chris Coble and John Wimmer, of Lilly Endowment Inc., and James Lewis, of the Louisville Institute.

And, most important, to the worshipers and their congregations who generously gave their time to help us explore the promise of place.

Location, location, location?
Test your assumptions.

Introduction

I believe in looking reality straight in the eye and denying it.

GARRISON KEILLOR

Surprising and vexing facts fill the pages of this book. We propose no eloquent theories or one-size-fits-all recommendations about location. We labored to harness complex data so that reality could speak for itself. The reality is that *good ministry happens everywhere* when congregations see their location as a gift, promise, and strength.

In this book we test long-standing assumptions about the role of location in determining the vitality achieved by congregations. A congregation's internal characteristics share a multifaceted relationship with its location. To explain clearly the role of location requires knowing what is going on in the congregation. Then, the influence of internal factors must be compared with the power of community factors. Some neighborhood characteristics turn out to be quite powerful and worth understanding in depth. Other area traits prove to be irrelevant for achieving congregational strength. Congregations can achieve particular strength when their ministry focus and leadership decisions are tailored to the community. In the coming chapters, we lay out a new situational model for congregations ready to see their place as another God-given strength.

Much social science research emphasizes the overwhelming influence of community factors on congregational life. From this perspective, the congregation's context determines who they *have been*, what they currently *are*, and what their *future* holds. Many researchers see community demographics (population change, age profiles, types of families, and economic needs) as powerful determinants of a congregation's effectiveness and numerical growth. This point of view claims that knowing the surrounding area is essential for perceiving what the future holds for the congregation. Church growth studies presumed that, as goes the neighborhood, so goes the church.[1] While noting the role of internal factors, these studies often directed leaders to pay attention to external features outside the congregation's doors, and thus, outside their control.

The challenge of untangling the relationship between location and congregational vitality proved more difficult than we expected. The research process resembled the way a kaleidoscope works. Kaleidoscopes contain tiny pieces of colored glass. A cylindrical tube with mirrors lets the viewer see the colored glass shards in a new way—through a prism. With each turn of the cylinder, the bits of glass move, revealing new geometric patterns. The greater the number of glass pieces, the larger the number of possible patterns. With even a dozen glass pieces, the mathematical possibilities for unique patterns dramatically escalate.[2] This image captures the intricacy of our task. First, what are the glass pieces—the pieces of contextual information congregations need to identify? Second, can the general patterns of community context and ministry focus be described accurately? If so, can congregations rotate the prism of research findings to understand and build on their unique combination of place and ministry?

In summary, this book:

- tests the myth that a congregation's vitality is determined by its community context

- asserts that *every* congregation has a dynamic relationship with the community where it is located

- provides evidence that *every* congregation can achieve strength and effectiveness in its present location

- shows the extent to which congregational effectiveness and numerical growth are dependent on the fit between ministry focus and factors external to the congregation

- demonstrates that congregations can fail to achieve a high level of effectiveness if their leaders judge some community factors to be powerful when they are in fact irrelevant to congregational strength

- demonstrates that congregations can fail to achieve a high level of effectiveness if their leaders judge some community factors to be irrelevant when they are in fact powerful in achieving congregational vitality

- creates a map to help congregational leaders distinguish between relevant and irrelevant community factors.

Place as Strength

In *Beyond the Ordinary: Ten Strengths of U.S. Congregations*, we detailed ten important aspects of congregational vitality.[3] There, we focused on strengths—believing that naming what makes congregations strong fosters more improvement than identifying weaknesses. Changing the mindset from "what's wrong with us" to "what's right with us" moves congregations toward greater effectiveness. This shift celebrates the positives in congregational life and motivates worshipers and leaders to take necessary actions. Building on strength supplies the leverage for the next steps of a congregation's future. Our research demonstrates that all congregations have strengths.

We also target more than one measure of vital congregational life. Too often church consultants or denominational and congregational leaders stress one measure of success—numerical growth. Yet we found healthy congregations in many places, despite a relatively stable number of worshipers. Each of the ten strengths contributes to the health and vitality of individual congregations.

What are the ten factors that are important for successful congregations? Strong congregations: (1) help their worshipers grow spiritually, (2) provide meaningful worship, (3) are places where worshipers participate in the congregation in many ways, (4) give worshipers a sense of belonging, (5) care for children and youth, (6) focus on the community, (7) help worshipers share their faith with others, (8) welcome new people, (9) rely on empowering congregational leadership, and (10) have a positive outlook on the future. These strengths are calculated from the responses of all worshipers in the more than 2,000 congregations that participated in the U.S. Congregational Life Survey. The U.S. Congregational Life Survey, conducted in April 2001, provides unique insights. Many previous studies of congregational life either take a case-study approach—viewing a small number of congregations at a time—or rely on the views of one person—typically the minister, pastor, priest, rabbi, or other key leader. Instead, everyone fifteen years of age or older attending worship in congregations participating in the U.S. Congregational Life Survey responded to about fifty survey questions. This scientific, national random sample of congregations and their worshipers offers a new avenue for exploring the intersection of location and vitality. (For more information about the U.S. Congregational Life Survey see appendixes 2 and 3.)

The strength measurements that tap each dimension rely on multiple survey questions (with one exception). Because the calculations stem from the input of many worshipers and use responses to multiple questions, they generate robust measures of congregational strength.[4]

Beyond the Ordinary summarized how these strengths play out in congregations of different sizes, from different faith groups, and with worshipers whose average age is older or younger than the national average.

What Do We Mean by Location?

Where is your congregation located? How can we describe the congregation's geography in very broad ways, such as the region of the country, and in the most local way, the neighborhood? Do congregations in different types of places have different strengths? How do congregations interact with their communities? These questions can be answered in many ways. The following chapters examine how location influences congregational life, using different approaches.

TEN STRENGTHS
OF CONGREGATIONS

Growing Spiritually: Where many worshipers are growing in their faith and feel the congregation meets their spiritual needs

Meaningful Worship: Where many worshipers experience God's presence, joy, inspiration, and awe in worship services and feel worship helps them with everyday life

Participating in the Congregation: Where many worshipers attend services weekly and are involved in the congregation in other ways

Sense of Belonging: Where many worshipers have a strong sense of belonging and say most of their closest friends attend the same congregation

Caring for Children and Youth: Where many worshipers are satisfied with the offerings for children and youth and have children living at home who also attend there

Focusing on the Community: Where many worshipers are involved in social service or advocacy activities and work to make their community a better place to live

Sharing Faith: Where many worshipers are involved in evangelism activities and invite friends or relatives to worship

Welcoming New People: Where many worshipers began attending in the past five years

Empowering Leadership: Where many worshipers feel the congregation's leaders inspire others to action and take into account worshipers' ideas

Looking to the Future: Where many worshipers feel committed to the congregation's vision and are excited about the congregation's future

From *Beyond the Ordinary: Ten Strengths of U.S. Congregations*, by Cynthia Woolever and Deborah Bruce (Louisville, KY: Westminster John Knox Press, 2004).

First, location can be defined geographically based on region—is your congregation located in the Northeast, South, Midwest, or West? The U.S. Census defines these four regions. Everyone from government statisticians to economic analysts to researchers in a variety of fields use them to distinguish between the country's major geographic areas. In chapter 1, we look at whether the strengths of congregations in these geographic regions differ. Do congregations in the Midwest, for example, excel in specific ways?

Second, location can be defined geographically based on political stance—is your congregation located in a "red" or "blue" state? These labels emerged during recent presidential elections. As media outlets tracked early election returns on U.S. maps, states where a majority voted for the Republican candidate were shown in red, and those where a majority voted for the Democratic candidate were shown in blue. These terms have become shorthand ways of referring to Republican and Democratic or Conservative and Liberal differences. Red and blue states follow clear geographic patterns. Blue states are in the Northeast, on the Pacific Coast, and in the upper Midwest; red states are the remaining states. Yet it is helpful to remember that not all voters in red states voted for the Republican candidate and vice versa. For that reason, we also examine the red/blue divide at the county level. Does it make a difference if your congregation is located in a red county within a blue state, for example? We examine the relationship between the red/blue divide and congregational strengths in chapter 1.

Third, location can be defined geographically based on the role religion plays in your area. That is, is your congregation in the "Bible Belt" or not? This term is often used (positively and negatively) to refer to states, mostly in the South, where religion has a strong hold. In particular, evangelical or conservative Protestant views tend to prevail in the Bible Belt. Interestingly, the states included in what we refer to today as the Bible Belt overlap substantially with those that seceded from the United States to form the Confederacy. In that sense, the Bible Belt may reflect historical political differences, as well. Many southern cities claim to be the "buckle" of the Bible Belt. Chapter 2 illustrates the ways in which Bible Belt congregations stand out. Is there any truth to the idea of a Bible Belt?

Fourth, location can be defined religiously, based on the mix of religions and denominations in the area—is your congregation in a largely Catholic area or are many of the churches in your community Baptist or Mormon perhaps? Examining the congregations in your area and the percentage of people affiliated with faith communities reveals much about your congregation's "competition" in the religious sector (also described in chapter 2). The Religious Congregations and Membership Study (RCMS), conducted every ten years, describes the religious composition of every county in this country and provides estimates of the number of people in the county who are not affiliated with any religion.[5] In some communities, relatively few people are affiliated with a church, synagogue, mosque, or other faith community. In other places, most are. In chapter 2, we use RCMS data to look at the relationship between congregational strengths and the religious marketplace in which congregations operate. Does it make a difference if a Catholic church is the only one in town or is one of many parishes?

MYTH TRAPS

Myths are tempting assumptions about congregational life. Myths lure us to beliefs that we want to be true. Believing myths is its own reward. Myths allow us to avoid change and permit us to use the same old methods to get the same old results. Myths immobilize and trap us in dead ends, blocking us from fully living out the answer to our most important question: What is God calling us to be and do as a congregation?

Fifth, location can be defined demographically—how can we describe the people living in the community around your congregation? The U.S. Census provides voluminous information that can help describe communities—the age, gender, education level, income, and occupation of the residents; the types of housing; the prevalence of poverty and crime; and the population growth. In chapter 3, we consider the relationship between the types of people living around a congregation and the strengths that congregation can claim. Are congregations located in areas with many children living at home particularly good at serving the needs of children and youth?

Location can also be considered demographically by focusing on the match between your worshipers and particular segments of the local population (for example, traditional families). Do your worshipers "match" the people living in the community around your congregation? This match can be assessed on many of the dimensions included in the U.S. Census—age, race, and marital status, for example. Chapter 4 shows how congregations that fit their communities compare to those that don't. Do congregations whose worshipers closely mirror the types of people in the local community do better at focusing on their communities, for example?

Finally, chapter 5 combines these different ways of conceptualizing location. We examine the relative influence of each in predicting congregational strength and numerical growth. For example, which is more helpful for predicting growth or vitality—knowing the region where a congregation is located or the types of people who live in the neighborhood?

What Model Drives Our Congregation's Thinking?

The time-worn phrase—the three principles of real estate success are "location, location, location"—echoes a marketplace understanding of a site's value. As congregations assess their location, do the secular criteria of real estate evaluation apply? For instance, how much should land values, future use, available parking, new construction, or accessibility to highways influence leaders' thinking? Should leaders appraise their congregation's location in the same way that business owners and corporations evaluate potential locations for a retail outlet, shopping mall, or new apartment complex?

Communities of faith draw from a deeper well of values. For most congregations the past conveys significant religious meaning. Worshipers and leaders believe God founded their church, parish, or congregation at a particular moment in history, on a particular spot on the globe. Further, visionary leaders often recount the specificity of this beginning in time and space through a powerful story. This view asserts that the place claims the congregation as much as the congregation claims the place.

A local congregation's "birth story" bestows a unique birthright as well. The biblical story of Esau tells about the loss of something priceless and irreplaceable—his birthright. As the eldest son, Esau stands to receive his birthright—his father's property and his place in the family lineage. Unfortunately, Esau sells his birthright for a bowl of soup. He freely makes the tragic choice to give up his priceless inheritance in exchange for satisfying a momentary hunger. Part of this story's power arises from the illogical and unwise decision to sell a birthright, treating it like any other market commodity. A birthright comes as "an inherited identity" and carries "an obligation to use it, take care of it, pass it on, and hopefully improve it."[6] Likewise, a congregation's birthplace grants it a unique birthright, a nonreturnable gift meant only for this faith community.

While a birthright cannot be forcibly taken, it can be given or contracted away. Congregations loosen their grip on their location as a unique birthright when they fail to recognize their one-of-a-kind local heritage. When congregations do not see their location as a unique gift, they begin to feel their place is a negotiable commodity. They can begin to see their location as a material good for which there are a number of equally available and satisfying substitutes. Claiming the power of place means seeing the incalculable worth of a congregation's location. Leaders claim that power when they more fully understand what this gift offers. Leaders who judge some community characteristics as quite powerful when they are in fact irrelevant to achieving vitality settle for soup instead of something God-given and priceless.

What's a Nice Congregation like Ours Doing in a Place like This?

Why would God choose a pessimist to perform one of history's most optimistic actions? The biblical Jeremiah, who was hardly a glass-is-half-full kind of guy, earned his reputation as "the weeping prophet." Jeremiah 32 describes the scene of his unusual transactions. Jeremiah sat in jail as the Babylonians stormed Jerusalem. As his kingdom of Judah is about to be overthrown, Jeremiah receives "a word from God" commanding him to buy a piece of land in the heart of Jerusalem. At God's request, Jeremiah buys property in the worst possible real estate market—in the middle of a city about to be destroyed. Talking with his real estate agent instead of packing his bags, Jeremiah signs the deed while a crowd watches. "What is he doing? Is he crazy?" they must have murmured. We can conclude that:

> Jeremiah makes a downpayment on behalf of God . . . as a sign that God will redeem the people whose lives have been destroyed. The worst they could ever imagine is going to come to pass. Their city will be devastated. Their land will be

taken. The temple will be destroyed. They will be taken to live in a land that is not their own. But God makes a promise to bring them back. God makes a promise there will be a new day, when life in the land and hope in their hearts is restored.[7]

God calls congregations to pick up the shattered pieces and make something holy of them, to be in those places that the world sees as unlikely and unpromising. Some are called to ministry in locations of apparent promise. But for others, claiming their birthright means "buying real estate" on behalf of God in challenging locations and every corner of the earth. All of these are God's places of promise.

Explore the diverse religious landscape.

CHAPTER 1

STRENGTH IN STATES AND REGIONS

Tell me the landscape in which you live and I will tell you who you are.

JOSÉ ORTEGA Y GASSET

America's regions serve as sources of pride and personal reference. *"Where are you from?"* helps us locate people in their biographical story. Each region reflects differences—some apparent (topography or type of community) and some nuanced (dialect). Religious differences also make regions unique. As our ancestors moved across the frontier, their religious beliefs and organizations moved with them. In what ways do congregations reflect the social, cultural, and political traits prevalent in U.S. regions? Does location—the region where a congregation carries out its mission—determine the congregation's ministry effectiveness?

Northeast, West, and Places In Between

The U.S. Census Bureau neatly divides the country into four regions (see map 1.1). The Northeast includes roughly the states from Pennsylvania to Maine. The Midwest encompasses the middle states from the Dakotas to Ohio. The South reaches from Texas and Oklahoma up to the Virginias and Maryland. Finally, the West captures the remaining

NORTHEAST

Connecticut, Maine, Massachusetts, New Hampshire, New Jersey, New York, Pennsylvania, Rhode Island, Vermont

Catholics are the largest group of adherents in this region (38% of the population). Nearly half of the Jews in the country reside here as well.*

MIDWEST

Illinois, Indiana, Iowa, Kansas, Michigan, Minnesota, Missouri, Nebraska, North Dakota, Ohio, South Dakota, Wisconsin

Only in the Midwest are mainline Protestants and conservative Protestants equally represented in the churchgoing population. Lutherans and Methodists dominate among mainline churches.*

SOUTH

Alabama, Arkansas, Delaware, District of Columbia, Florida, Georgia, Kentucky, Louisiana, Maryland, Mississippi, North Carolina, Oklahoma, South Carolina, Tennessee, Texas, Virginia, West Virginia

Conservative Protestant adherents represent one in four people in this region. While many groups fit under the conservative Protestant umbrella, the Baptists and Assemblies of God are the two largest denominational groups in the South.*

WEST

Alaska, Arizona, California, Colorado, Hawaii, Idaho, Montana, Nevada, New Mexico, Oregon, Utah, Washington, Wyoming

The West is a diverse region where the most highly "churched" state in the country (Utah) sits in the midst of states with much lower rates of churchgoing. Another standout state is California, where the growing Latino population fuels attendance in Catholic parishes (70% of U.S. Latinos are Catholic).**

Religious Congregations and Membership in the United States 2000.

**Paul Perl, Jennifer Z. Greely, and Mark M. Gray, "What Percentage of Adult Hispanics Are Catholic? A Review of Survey Data and Methodology," *Journal for the Scientific Study of Religion,* September 2006, 419–36 (previous version available at: http://cara.georgetown.edu/Hispanic%20Catholics.pdf).

states, from mountainous Colorado to California and from New Mexico to Washington State. In addition, the West region takes in Alaska and Hawaii. The census further subdivides the four regions into smaller clusters of states (called divisions). For example, the Midwest Region, with twelve states, covers two divisions—West North Central with seven states and East North Central with five states.

In table 1.1 we list the four census regions and nine divisions with population figures.[1] More than one-third of the U.S. population lives in the South (36%). The Midwest

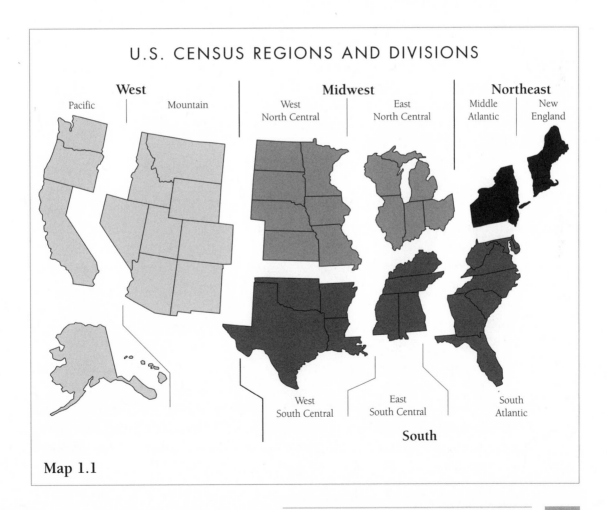

U.S. CENSUS REGIONS AND DIVISIONS

West — Pacific | Mountain

Midwest — West North Central | East North Central

Northeast — Middle Atlantic | New England

West South Central | East South Central | South Atlantic

South

Map 1.1

and West regions contain comparable numbers of people (23% and 22% of the U.S. population, respectively). Surprisingly, the dense Northeast comprises only about 19% of the country's total population.

While the U.S. Census gathers no information about religion, another national survey does (shown in the five columns to the right in table 1.1).[2] Catholics represent the largest faith group in the United States, claiming 22% of the population. Conservative Protestants take in about 14% of the population, followed by mainline Protestant churches reporting 9% of the population as adherents.[3] Orthodox and non-Christian worshipers make up a tiny proportion of the population—only 4.8%. Almost half of the U.S. population remains unaffiliated with any religious body.

The three largest faith groups—Catholics, conservative Protestants, and mainline Protestants—vary in the percentage of the population that they report as their adherents in the four census regions (see table 1.1). Catholics climb to 38% of the population in the Northeast region. In the South, conservative Protestant adherents almost double in their proportionate size, representing one in four people. Mainline Protestant figures change more modestly by region, but still rise to 13% of the population in the Midwest.[4]

Moving from regions to states, we see that Catholic adherents concentrate in four areas of the United States (see map 1.2). The U.S. map for Catholics shows the ten states with the highest percentages of Catholic adherents (dark gray shading) and the ten states with the second highest percentages of Catholics (light gray shading). The Northeast, with the highest concentration, was a final destination for many Italian and Irish Catholic immigrants. A second cluster of states—including Illinois, Wisconsin, Minnesota, and Michigan—hosts another wave of Catholic immigrants, usually German, French, or Polish. Finally, higher concentrations of Catholics also live in the Southwest—New Mexico, Texas, and California. Many Catholics in these states are Hispanic.

Many mainline Protestant churches and participants—Lutherans, Methodists, Presbyterians, and others—can be counted in other states (see map 1.3). Their geographic strength lies in the upper Midwest and along the Atlantic coast, involving states in the Middle and South Atlantic census divisions. While their roots are also European, immigrants to these areas settled the frontier, carrying their ancestors' religious commitments with them.

U.S. POPULATION AND FAITH GROUPS BY REGION AND DIVISIONS

REGION Division	Population*			Percentage of Population by Faith Group**				
	Population	% of U.S. Population	Total % Churched Population	Catholics	Mainline Protestants	Conservative Protestants	Other
NORTHEAST	53,594,378	**19%**	**59%**	**38%**	**9%**	**3%**	**9%**
New England	13,922,517	5%	57%	42%	8%	2%	5%
Middle Atlantic	39,671,861	14%	59%	37%	10%	4%	8%
MIDWEST	53,392,776	**23%**	**51%**	**22%**	**13%**	**13%**	**3%**
East North Central	45,155,037	16%	49%	24%	11%	11%	3%
West North Central	19,237,739	7%	57%	20%	19%	16%	2%
SOUTH	100,236,820	**36%**	**49%**	**12%**	**10%**	**25%**	**2%**
South Atlantic	51,769,160	18%	43%	10%	11%	19%	3%
East South Central	17,022,810	6%	53%	5%	10%	38%	1%
West South Central	31,444,850	11%	57%	19%	8%	27%	3%
WEST	63,197,932	**22%**	**44%**	**23%**	**4%**	**8%**	**9%**
Mountain	18,172,295	6%	46%	18%	5%	9%	14%
Pacific	45,025,637	16%	43%	25%	4%	8%	6%
UNITED STATES	281,421,906	100%	**50%**	**22%**	**9%**	**14%**	**5%**

* Source: 2000 U.S. Census.

** Source: *Religious Congregations and Membership in the United States 2000* (Nashville: Glenmary Research Center). Percentages may not add to 100 due to rounding.

Table 1.1

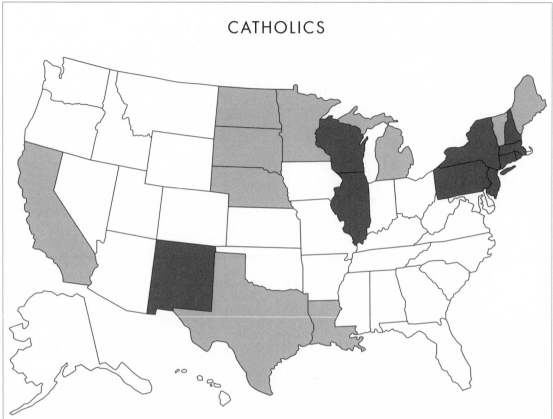

CATHOLICS

Note: Dark gray identifies the states with the highest percentages of adherents. Light gray identifies the states with the next highest percentages of adherents.

Map 1.2

Conservative Protestants reveal an entirely different distribution (see map 1.4). They are concentrated in twenty states located primarily in the South. While many groups are included under the umbrella of conservative Protestants, the Baptists and Assemblies of God dominate in the South. Conservative Protestant roots rest in American soil, with most groups beginning in rural areas.

Given the striking differences in the geographical distribution of these three faith groups, we wonder if there are regional effects on congregational life. Do people in some regions of the country favor certain congregational characteristics, programs, or theologies over others? Are some regions more likely to foster particular patterns of effectiveness in congregations?

Regions and congregational strength: Strengths exist in every congregation. We identified ten strengths that surface frequently across congregations of various sizes and

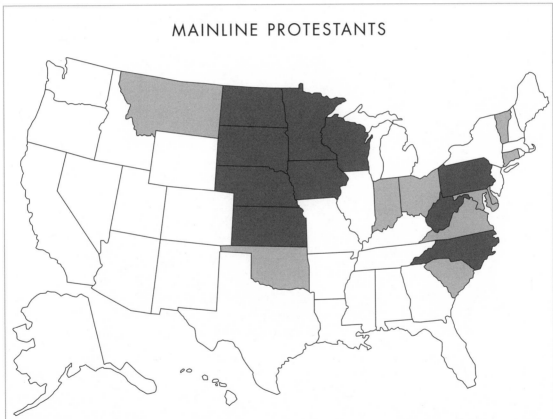

MAINLINE PROTESTANTS

Note: Dark gray identifies the states with the highest percentages of adherents. Light gray identifies the states with the next highest percentages of adherents.

Map 1.3

traditions.[5] A congregational strength operates as a powerful organizational dynamic, often driving or emerging from the mission focus of the congregation. Strengths become even more powerful when the congregation's leaders and worshipers consciously leverage them. Do congregational strengths emerge from a particular location or context? Are some strengths really "regional effects" masquerading as a congregational dynamic?

CONSERVATIVE PROTESTANTS

Note: Dark gray identifies the ten states with the highest percentages of adherents. Light gray identifies the ten states with the next highest percentages of adherents.

Map 1.4

We measured each of the ten strengths, using aggregated survey responses from worshipers in each congregation. Congregational scores on each strength measure could range between 0 and 100. No congregation achieves a perfect score of 100 or a failing score of zero. For example, on the first measure, the Growing Spiritually Index, the typical congregation scores 47. (See appendix 4 for a complete list of items in each strength index and the U.S. average for all congregations.) While a single congregation can have multiple strengths, no congregation excels on all ten strengths. A typical congregation does well in three to five ministry areas.

Table 1.2 shows the average strength scores for congregations in each of the four U.S. Census regions. Numbers in bold show where the average strength scores for congregations in one region are *higher* than for other congregations. Remember that these are just averages: individual congregations may score much higher or lower than their regional averages. Since nine out of the ten strengths have one or more regional scores in bold, the table illustrates a clear pattern of diverse strengths across regions of the country. For example, congregations located in the South, known for its religiosity and love of the Bible, excel in six out of ten strengths: two spiritual strengths (Growing Spiritually and Meaningful Worship), one internal strength (Participating in the Congregation), one external strength (Sharing Faith), and two leadership strengths (Empowering Leadership and Looking to the Future).

Congregations in the Midwest region also excel in multiple areas of strength. They boast four of the same strengths that southern congregations typically claim, but they do well on the Sense of Belonging Index too. Yet Midwest congregations don't score as high as those in the South in Sharing Faith or Looking to the Future.

Congregations in the Northeast typically claim only one overall strength—Focusing on the Community. Congregations located in the West also claim only one strength—Welcoming New People. In part, this type of strength stems from congregations successfully responding to the West's high population growth and mobility rates. Looking across these patterns tells us that congregations in every region of the country have developed strengths.

We calculated a composite measure of congregational strength—simply the average score across all ten individual strength indexes. The total congregational vitality

TEN STRENGTHS, OVERALL VITALITY, AND U.S. CENSUS REGIONS

STRENGTHS	NORTH-EAST	MID-WEST	SOUTH	WEST	NORTH-EAST	MID-WEST	SOUTH	WEST
	TOTAL				CATHOLIC			
1 Growing Spiritually	41	**50**	**49**	43	37	40	38	38
2 Meaningful Worship	56	**65**	**65**	57	54	60	63	56
3 Participating in the Congregation	54	**63**	**63**	54	43	48	42	44
4 Sense of Belonging	32	**40**	37	33	29	29	31	30
5 Caring for Children and Youth	53	52	49	49	43	46	47	47
6 Focusing on the Community	**37**	31	32	34	31	34	28	35
7 Sharing Faith	23	33	**37**	28	20	18	21	21
8 Welcoming New People	27	34	33	**39**	25	19	**40**	27
9 Empowering Leadership	47	**51**	**53**	39	43	42	44	32
10 Looking to the Future	38	41	**43**	37	35	35	35	32
Overall Vitality	41	**44**	**46**	41	36	37	37	36
	MAINLINE PROTESTANT				CONSERVATIVE PROTESTANT			
1 Growing Spiritually	40	42	41	39	51	**57**	**56**	51
2 Meaningful Worship	55	56	58	52	60	**71**	**70**	63
3 Participating in the Congregation	54	55	55	53	62	**70**	**71**	61
4 Sense of Belonging	31	30	31	28	38	**47**	42	38
5 Caring for Children and Youth	**54**	**53**	46	45	60	53	52	53
6 Focusing on the Community	41	37	37	40	30	27	28	29
7 Sharing Faith	21	22	**26**	21	33	42	**47**	38
8 Welcoming New People	26	26	30	34	30	42	34	**51**
9 Empowering Leadership	46	44	44	38	53	57	**60**	45
10 Looking to the Future	38	35	35	32	44	46	48	44
Overall Vitality	40	40	40	38	46	48	50	47

Note: All values presented in the table are (weighted) means. Bold numbers indicate high scores for strengths where the mean differences between scores are statistically significant (at the $p < .05$ level or less). More information about the denominational families used here and throughout the book is available in appendix 5.

Table 1.2

score for congregations in each region also appears in table 1.2. Again, congregations in the South and Midwest reach the higher overall scores. Lower total vitality scores occur in congregations located in the Northeast and West. These scores reflect averages—many congregations score higher or lower in every region. Thus, individual congregations in a particular region may be more vital or less effective than other congregations in the region.

Faith groups and region: Many of these regional differences fade when they are examined within particular faith groups. For example, the only strength that shows a regional difference among Catholic parishes is Welcoming New People. Catholic parishes in the South excel at Welcoming New People, while Catholic parishes in other U.S. regions score lower. In a similar way, mainline Protestant congregations show relatively few differences by region. Mainline Protestant churches in the Northeast and Midwest are more likely to excel in Caring for Children and Youth, while those in the South lean toward excellence in Sharing Faith.

However, conservative Protestant congregations appear to experience far more regional influences than other faith groups. Seven out of ten strengths are significantly linked to region among such churches. Conservative Protestant churches in the Midwest and South tend to be stronger in Growing Spiritually, Meaningful Worship, and Participating in the Congregation. The strength of having a Sense of Belonging surfaces more often in the Midwest. Conservative Protestant churches in the South outscore such churches located elsewhere on Sharing Faith and Empowering Leadership. Welcoming New People scores are highest for conservative Protestant churches in the West. Conservative Protestant churches in the Northeast reveal no significant advantage over similar churches in other regions.

Looking across all of the comparisons in table 1.2 tells us that a multiple-strength congregation is most likely to surface among conservative Protestant churches in the South. They excel, on average, in five of the ten strengths. Region has a much smaller impact on churches in other faith groups.

Red and Blue Religion

Color-coding states during national elections began with color television in the 1960s. But it was not until the highly contested 2000 presidential election that all the networks started using the same colors. The practice of designating a state by a single color comes from a political system in which the candidate getting the most votes in a state becomes the winner-take-all of the electoral votes (used in forty-eight of the fifty states). The networks chose red to indicate the states that went for George W. Bush (Republican) and blue to show the states won by Al Gore (Democrat). Because it took months to settle officially who won the election, Americans repeatedly saw the same red and blue map. Because of this shared national experience, the labels "red state" and "blue state" entered the language. In the 2004 election only three states (New Mexico, Iowa, and New Hampshire) changed color. Therefore, many analysts linked the red-state/blue-state divide to other issues and enduring behaviors.[6] Red state implies a more conservative, rural region. Blue state suggests a more urban, multicultural, and liberal region (see map 1.5).

Red and blue states and congregational strengths: Congregations in red states show far more strengths than blue-state congregations (see table 1.3). They possess greater effectiveness in seven out of the ten strengths: two spiritual strengths (Growing Spiritually and Meaningful Worship), two internal strengths (Participating in the Congregation and Sense of Belonging), one external strength (Sharing Faith), and two leadership strengths (Empowering Leadership and Looking to the Future). Congregations in blue states out-power congregations in red states on only one strength—Focusing on the Community. Overall vitality scores rise to higher levels in red-state congregations.

Faith group and the red-state/blue-state divide: A closer look at the red-state/blue-state divide among Catholic parishes shows that the strengths of these congregations differ by state type. Bucking the national trend, Catholic parishes in red states outscore their sister parishes in blue states on Caring for Children and Youth. But blue-state Catholic parishes lead the way on another strength—Empowering Leadership. Further differences are not reflected among Catholic parishes.

Few of the overall red-state/blue-state differences filter down to mainline Protestant

BLUE STATES VERSUS RED STATES

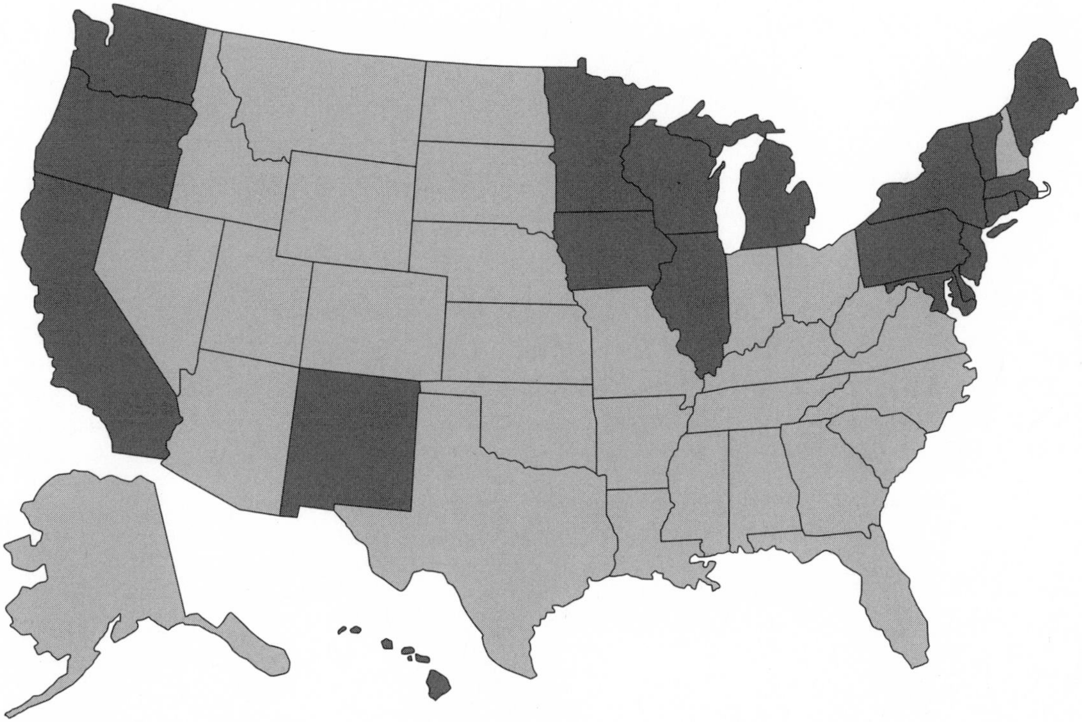

Note: Dark gray indicates "blue states," where Kerry (Democrat) won the majority of electoral votes in the 2004 presidential election.

Light gray indicates "red states," where Bush (Republican) won the majority of electoral votes in the 2004 presidential election.

Map 1.5

churches. On average, mainline Protestant churches in blue states score higher than those in red states on Caring for Children and Youth. On the other hand, mainline Protestant churches in red states excel in Sharing Faith.

When it comes to conservative Protestant churches, the red-state advantage seen in the overall scores remains. In six out of the ten strengths, red-state conservative

TEN STRENGTHS, OVERALL VITALITY, AND RED/BLUE STATES

STRENGTHS	TOTAL		CATHOLIC		MAINLINE PROTESTANT		CONSERVATIVE PROTESTANT	
	Blue	Red	Blue	Red	Blue	Red	Blue	Red
1 Growing Spiritually	44	**49**	39	37	40	41	53	**56**
2 Meaningful Worship	58	**64**	57	58	55	57	65	**70**
3 Participating in the Congregation	54	**63**	44	44	54	55	62	**71**
4 Sense of Belonging	33	**38**	31	29	30	31	38	**44**
5 Caring for Children and Youth	49	51	42	**48**	**51**	47	51	54
6 Focusing on the Community	**36**	31	33	32	39	37	30	28
7 Sharing Faith	25	**36**	21	19	21	**25**	34	**46**
8 Welcoming New People	32	34	25	28	27	30	42	38
9 Empowering Leadership	46	**51**	**43**	35	45	42	50	**58**
10 Looking to the Future	38	**42**	35	33	35	35	44	47
Overall Vitality	42	**45**	37	36	40	40	47	**50**

Blue = States where Kerry (Democrat) won the majority of electoral votes in the 2004 presidential election.
Red = States where Bush (Republican) won the majority of electoral votes in the 2004 presidential election.
Note: All values presented in the table are (weighted) means. Bold numbers indicate high scores for strengths where the mean differences between scores are statistically significant (at the $p < .05$ level or less).

Table 1.3

MYTH TRAP

Congregations affiliated with the major U.S. denominations are uniformly spread across the country.

Many people think that—because every American community has Catholics, Methodists, and so on—every effective congregation *operates in the same context.* Not so!

Dispersion: Of 149 major U.S. religious bodies, only twenty denominational groups (including Muslims and Jews) reported adherents in all fifty states and the District of Columbia.

Concentration: But many of these twenty groups' adherents are highly concentrated geographically. *All twenty groups* report that at least half of their adherents live in just ten states. Note the major differences in dispersion and concentration:

- United Methodists and Assemblies of God are the *least* concentrated (54% of their adherents reside in just ten states).
- Other groups are slightly more concentrated—Nazarenes and Presbyterians (57% and 58% of adherents, respectively, reside in just ten states).
- Much more concentrated than other groups are Catholics and Southern Baptists (69% and 74% of adherents, respectively, reside in just ten states).
- Jews are *most* concentrated (82% of adherents reside in just ten states), with Mormons following close behind (78% of adherents reside in just ten states).*

The dispersion-concentration factor influences *how adherents feel:* Adherents in low-concentration areas of "our denomination" can feel like outsiders in an alien culture. At the same time, such a "minority" status may fuel a strong, distinctive congregational identity that clarifies ministry focus.

In what ways does your part of the country influence how worshipers feel about their affiliation with your congregation?

*Data from *Religious Congregations and Membership in the United States 2000;* analyses by Dale Jones, Church Growth Research Center, Church of the Nazarene (e-mail message to authors, April 7, 2006).

Protestant churches flex more congregational strength than similar blue-state churches. The six include two spiritual strengths (Growing Spiritually and Meaningful Worship), two strengths internal to the congregation (Participating in the Congregation and Sense of Belonging), Sharing Faith, and Empowering Leadership.

Faith group and the red-county/blue-county divide: Just as states can be identified as red or blue based on who won the majority of votes, individual counties can also be designated as red or blue based on whether the Democratic or Republican candidate won the majority of votes. Do the patterns of strength at the state level hold true when we look at voting patterns at the county level? In fact, congregational strengths at the county level follow many of the same patterns as in red or blue states. Red-county congregations, like red-state congregations, show more strength than blue-county congregations (see table 1.4). However, when the focus shifts to the county level, the red/blue divide we saw for three other measures disappears: Empowering Leadership, Looking to the Future, and the Overall Vitality Index. Counties are smaller geographic units than states, reflecting finer subcultural distinctions and voting results. Moving to the county-level measurement of the red/blue divide produces other exceptions. Focusing on the Community and Welcoming New People appear as strengths for congregations located in blue counties.

At the county level, Catholic parishes do not differ in their congregational strengths by a blue or red designation. Mainline Protestant churches reveal more red/blue differences at the county level. Blue-county mainline Protestant churches score significantly higher in three areas (vs. only two areas at the state level): Focusing on the Community, Welcoming New People, and Empowering Leadership. In five instances (vs. six at the state level), red-county conservative Protestant churches continue to outscore similar blue-county churches in spiritual, internal, and external strengths (Growing Spiritually, Meaningful Worship, Participating in the Congregation, Sense of Belonging, and Sharing Faith). Blue-county conservative Protestant churches do better than similar red-county churches at Welcoming New People. The faith group differences disappear on the overall vitality measure at the county level.

Blue county in red state and red county in blue state: Some counties do not follow their state's voting pattern—for example, a county that voted for Gore in a state that voted for Bush. What happens when a blue county is part of a red state? Do congregational strengths differ if a congregation is located in a red county in a blue state? Our analysis also shows that a red-county, red-state location maintains the congregational strength advantage. For seven out of ten strengths and the Overall Vitality Index,

TEN STRENGTHS, OVERALL VITALITY, AND RED/BLUE COUNTIES

STRENGTHS	TOTAL		CATHOLIC		MAINLINE PROTESTANT		CONSERVATIVE PROTESTANT	
	Blue	Red	Blue	Red	Blue	Red	Blue	Red
1 Growing Spiritually	43	**49**	38	38	39	41	51	**56**
2 Meaningful Worship	58	**64**	56	59	55	57	65	**70**
3 Participating in the Congregation	55	**62**	44	45	54	55	63	**70**
4 Sense of Belonging	33	**38**	32	28	32	30	37	**44**
5 Caring for Children and Youth	50	51	44	48	51	49	52	53
6 Focusing on the Community	**36**	32	34	32	**42**	37	29	28
7 Sharing Faith	27	**35**	21	18	21	23	39	**44**
8 Welcoming New People	**37**	32	29	25	**33**	26	**48**	37
9 Empowering Leadership	47	50	42	36	**47**	42	51	58
10 Looking to the Future	40	41	35	33	38	34	47	47
Overall Vitality	42	44	37	35	41	39	47	49

Blue = Counties where Kerry (Democrat) won the majority of votes in the 2004 presidential election.

Red = Counties where Bush (Republican) won the majority of votes in the 2004 presidential election.

Note: All values presented in the table are (weighted) means. Bold numbers indicate high scores for strengths where the mean differences between scores are statistically significant (at the $p < .05$ level or less).

Table 1.4

MYTH TRAP

Effective congregations affiliated with major U.S. denominations provide the same ministries in the same ways in every state.

Many people think that—because every American community has Catholics, Methodists, and so on—every effective congregation *does the same ministries in the same ways.* Not so!

Each congregation ministers as a niche within its specific religious landscape. Each effective congregation's ministry strengths therefore differ from congregations of its faith family in other parts of the country.

The congregational dispersion-concentration factor influences *what effective congregations do:* Catholics are heavily concentrated in the Northeast, Texas, New Mexico, and California. A Protestant congregation located in a heavily Catholic area does effective ministry differently than does a Protestant congregation located in the South, where most congregations are Protestant. One example:

- In mainline churches in New England—United Methodist, United Church of Christ, and Presbyterian—the percentage of adult worshipers who attend church school classes is *quite low.* A large percentage of the religious adherents in New England states are Catholics, and this religious tradition seldom stresses the importance of adults attending church school classes. This de-emphasis on church school spills over to those attending mainline churches.

- By contrast, the percentage of adult worshipers in mainline churches who attend church school classes in the South is *quite high.* A large percentage of the religious adherents in Southern states are Southern Baptist, and this denomination encourages adults to attend church school classes. Again, this emphasis has an impact on mainline churches.

In what other way does your part of the country influence your congregation's ministries?

congregations in red-county/red-state locations achieve the highest levels of strength. Congregations in blue-county/blue-state locations have a single advantage. They outdistance congregations in other combinations of county-state types on the Focusing on the Community strength. Congregations located in blue counties within red states excel in Welcoming New People.

Faith group differences seen at the state and county level persist in a similar pattern in the county-state types. Just as Catholic parishes showed few differences at the county or state level, they exhibit few differences at the county-state level. Catholic parishes in blue counties located in blue states outscore parishes in other county-state types on having a Sense of Belonging.

Mainline Protestant churches in blue-county/blue-state areas excel in two external focus strengths—Focusing on the Community and Welcoming New People. Mainline Protestant churches in red-county/red-state areas excel in Sharing Faith.

Finally, conservative Protestant churches in red-county/red-state areas excel in six strengths and the Overall Vitality Index. A blue-county/red-state area remains the best location for congregational strength in Welcoming New People for conservative Protestant churches.

Finding Strength from North to South and Red to Blue

Using broad strokes, we paint a regional picture of congregational vitality that illustrates consistent patterns. Congregations in the Midwest, South, and red states and counties exhibit more vitality than congregations in other parts of the country. However, these patterns hold true primarily among conservative Protestant churches. Do successful congregations in the Midwest, South, red states, and red counties simply benefit from a context that is more consistent with their mission focus? It's possible. An equally plausible explanation describes congregations in red states, red counties, the South, and the Midwest as more responsive to their context. They focus their ministry in ways that meet the needs of people living in those places, spurred on by a more evangelical theology.

Congregations tend to be concentrated geographically according to their faith family. This geographic fact plays a role in how worshipers might perceive their location. But the concentration-dispersion factor also plays a role in effective ministry. Congregations in the same faith family but in different parts of the country will adopt different strategies to relate successfully to their community.

Why do broad geographic regions seem to play a smaller role in the strengths of Catholic parishes and mainline Protestant churches? This finding relates to what Catholic parishes and mainline Protestant churches typically emphasize that is consistent regardless of region. Certainly, the Catholic Church sees itself as a universal church, serving the entire world. Mainline Protestant churches claim European roots that channel their efforts based on traditions of the past. However, at their best, denominational theologies serve as "cultural handrails"—linking people to the past but also guiding them to a promising future.[7]

Cross the cultural divide.

CHAPTER 2

STRENGTH IN RELIGIOUS GEOGRAPHY

John Dunne says, "Those that see God see everything else."
I say: Those that learn to see everything else learn to see God.

JOAN CHITTISTER

"There are two types of people in the world," an old quip says. "Those who divide the world into two types and those who don't."[1] In the religious world, some people divide the country into two categories—the Bible Belt and everywhere else. Others divide people into two groups—churchgoers and everybody else.

Gary Farley alleges there are also two kinds of ecclesiologies—two visions of the church—in America.[2] One kind of church is "Made in America"—"sectarian, revivalistic crusaders."[3] The second kind of church claims a "European heritage"—often mainline Protestant churches. Churches of the second type, claims Farley, believe in a national church connection and emphasize serving people in the local community.

This chapter investigates two religious dichotomies. One is familiar—the Bible Belt versus the rest of the country—and one is not so familiar—highly churched versus less churched areas. And we investigate their relationship to congregational vitality. We compare Catholic parishes, mainline Protestant churches, and conservative Protestant churches in the Bible Belt to those located in other parts of the country. And we compare congregations in each faith family in highly churched areas to those in less churched areas.

Bible Belt Religion

Invented by sarcastic H. L. Mencken as he reported on the famous Scopes Trial in July 1925, the term *Bible Belt* describes a place where conservative religion and faith thrive. Mencken called the region around Dayton, Tennessee, where the trial was held, "this bright, shining, buckle of the Bible Belt."[4] Unfortunately, no precise definition indicates which states or counties fall within the belt.[5] Our analysis puts sixteen states in the Bible Belt, primarily southern states, stretching from Texas to the Virginias and from Florida to Kentucky (see map 2.1).[6] We compared U.S. Congregational Life Survey (U.S. CLS) congregations in these sixteen states to those outside the Bible Belt to assess the validity of common beliefs about Bible Belt religion.

The Bible Belt and congregational strengths: Congregations in the Bible Belt live up to their region's reputation (see the first few columns in table 2.1). In seven out of ten strengths, they outscore their sister congregations in other areas of the country. Bible Belt congregations excel on spiritual strengths (Growing Spiritually and Meaningful Worship), internal strengths (Participating in the Congregation and Sense of Belonging), one external strength (Sharing Faith), and leadership strengths (Empowering Leadership and Looking to the Future). Congregations outside the Bible Belt typically score higher than other congregations on only one strength—Focusing on the Community.

Faith groups and Bible Belt religion: Catholic parishes in the Bible Belt score higher on Welcoming New People, a difference not found when all faith groups in the Bible Belt are combined (see table 2.1). Bible Belt mainline Protestant churches gain advantage in Meaningful Worship and Caring for Children and Youth. But mainline Protestant churches in other areas of the country show greater strength in Sharing Faith. Finally, conservative Protestant churches in the Bible Belt score higher than conservative Protestant churches located outside the Bible Belt on Participating in the Congregation,

Caring for Children and Youth, Empowering Leadership, and Looking to the Future. Reflecting these spiritual areas of strength, scores on the overall vitality measure also stand out for conservative Protestant churches in the Bible Belt.

Being in the Bible Belt makes the biggest difference in vitality for conservative Protestant churches. These more theologically conservative churches thrive in the southern states where their mission closely reflects regional values such as individualism,

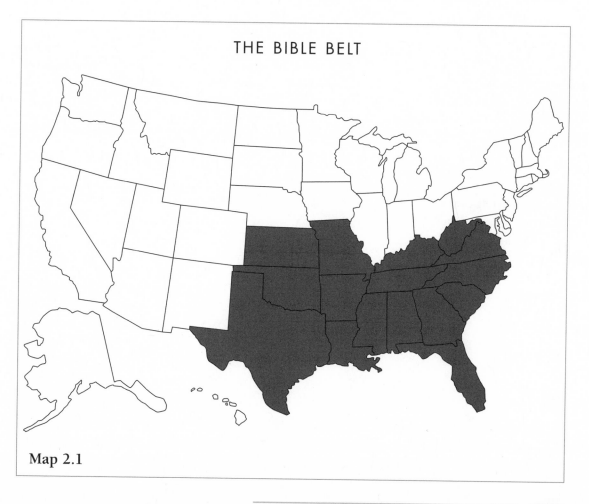

THE BIBLE BELT

Map 2.1

TEN STRENGTHS, OVERALL VITALITY, AND THE BIBLE BELT

STRENGTHS	TOTAL		CATHOLIC		MAINLINE PROTESTANT		CONSERVATIVE PROTESTANT	
	Bible Belt	Rest	Bible Belt	Rest	Bible Belt	Rest	Bible Belt	Rest
1 Growing Spiritually	**50**	45	38	38	41	40	56	54
2 Meaningful Worship	**65**	60	63	57	**58**	55	70	67
3 Participating in the Congregation	**64**	57	43	45	55	54	**71**	66
4 Sense of Belonging	**38**	35	32	30	31	30	43	43
5 Caring for Children and Youth	50	51	21	20	**26**	21	**46**	40
6 Focusing on the Community	31	**34**	29	34	38	39	28	28
7 Sharing Faith	**38**	28	47	45	46	**52**	53	53
8 Welcoming New People	33	34	**39**	24	30	27	34	**44**
9 Empowering Leadership	**54**	46	35	34	36	35	**49**	43
10 Looking to the Future	**44**	38	44	38	43	44	**61**	51
Overall Vitality	**46**	41	37	36	40	40	**51**	47

Note: All values presented in the table are (weighted) means. Bold numbers indicate high scores where the mean differences between scores are statistically significant (at the p < .05 level or less).

Table 2.1

reverence for the past, resistance to change, love of the land, a strong regional identity, an emphasis on family ties, and a close affinity between politics and religion.[7]

In contrast, Catholic parishes gain no boost in vitality from their presence in the Bible Belt. Mainline Protestant churches benefit in a few ways from their Bible Belt location, perhaps adopting some of the strategies of conservative churches in the region.

MYTH TRAP

Congregations around the country attract similar types of new people.

Our research shows that new people in congregations across the United States (people who began attending during the previous five years) fall into four categories:

- 9% are *first-timers* with no church background.
- 23% are *returnees* who were not attending anywhere before coming to their new congregation.
- 31% are *switchers* who changed denominations or faith groups.
- 38% are *transfers* who changed congregations within the same denomination.

Congregations in different areas attract different types of new people:

- Bible Belt congregations attract more switchers (38% of new worshipers) than those outside the Bible Belt (25%).
- Congregations outside the Bible Belt attract more first-timers (10%) and transfers (43%) than do those within the Bible Belt (7% first-timers; 31% transfers).

Do your congregation's strategies to attract new members address these facts?

A Religious Census

A coalition of religious researchers gathers information about religious organizations in every U.S. county every decade.[8] This census includes the number of people affiliated with each denomination or faith group in each county. By totaling up the number of affiliated people in the county and subtracting from the total county population, these researchers calculate the number of unaffiliated or "unclaimed" (what some groups refer to as "unchurched") in each county. From this religious census, we understand quite a bit about which denominations and faith groups are found in each county. For example, the census reveals that most urban counties contain a greater variety of religious groups than do rural ones; counties vary in the proportion of the population unaffiliated with congregations; and denominations vary widely in their regional distribution.[9]

This religious census shows that 22% of the U.S. population is affiliated with the Catholic Church. Reports from evangelical or conservative Protestant churches (from a large group of diverse denominations) reveal that 14% of the total population belongs to one of their congregations. Collective reports from mainline Protestant denominations indicate that about 9% of the population affiliates with one of their congregations. Across the country, 50% of the population is estimated to be unaffiliated with any denomination or faith group, though this figure differs substantially in different areas of the country (see table 1.1 on page 17 for affiliation rates by U.S. Census region and division).

"Churched" States and Counties

The percentages of people who are affiliated and unaffiliated with a congregation (sometimes called churched and unchurched) differ by county, state, and region (see map 2.2, showing most highly affiliated states). Parts of the Northeast, New Mexico, and Texas, with high percentages of Catholics, boast high affiliation rates—where a congregation of some kind claims almost 59% of the population. Utah exhibits a high affiliation rate because of the large percentage of Mormons living in the state. Some upper Midwestern states—Nebraska, the Dakotas, Minnesota, Iowa, and Wisconsin—also have high rates of affiliation. The affiliated in these states are more likely to be mainline Protestant churchgoers, primarily Lutheran. Western states have the lowest affiliation rates.

Churched counties and congregational strengths: In table 2.2 we show how congregational strengths link to opportunities for recruiting new worshipers—as measured

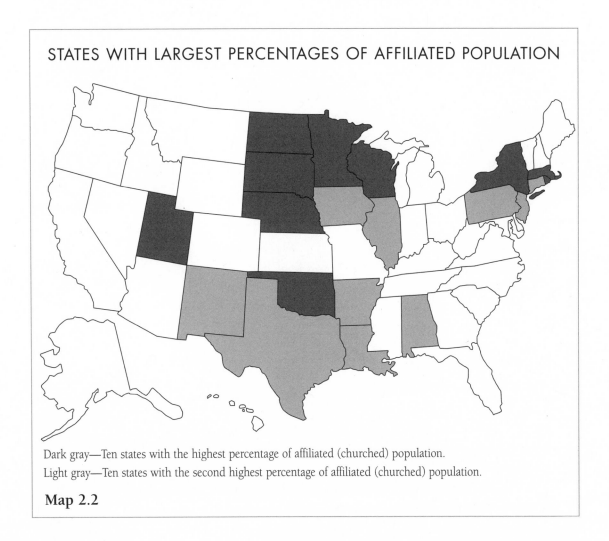

STATES WITH LARGEST PERCENTAGES OF AFFILIATED POPULATION

Dark gray—Ten states with the highest percentage of affiliated (churched) population.
Light gray—Ten states with the second highest percentage of affiliated (churched) population.

Map 2.2

TEN STRENGTHS, OVERALL VITALITY, AND PERCENT CHURCHED IN THE COUNTY

STRENGTHS	TOTAL	CATHOLIC	MAINLINE PROTESTANT	CONSERVATIVE PROTESTANT
1 Growing Spiritually	**.13**	.15	**.24**	**.16**
2 Meaningful Worship	**.12**	.28	**.18**	.06
3 Participating in the Congregation	**.11**	**.31**	.03	**.23**
4 Sense of Belonging	.07	-.00	.04	.11
5 Caring for Children and Youth	**.14**	.04	**.19**	.14
6 Focusing on the Community	**-.21**	-.10	**-.23**	**-.25**
7 Sharing Faith	.08	.06	.11	.12
8 Welcoming New People	**-.17**	**-.40**	**-.23**	-.12
9 Empowering Leadership	.05	-.09	.04	.11
10 Looking to the Future	.10	.08	-.04	**.23**
Overall Vitality	.05	.01	.04	.14

Note: A bold positive number indicates a significant positive correlation between the congregational strength and the percentage of the churched population in the county where the congregation is located (as the percentage of the churched population increases, congregations have higher strength scores).

A bold negative number indicates a significant negative correlation between the congregational strength and the percentage of the churched population in the county where the congregation is located (as the percentage of the churched population increases, congregations have lower strength scores).

All other correlations are not statistically significant.

Table 2.2

by the percentage of the local population that is unaffiliated with a congregation. If a county is above the national average in terms of the percentage of the population that is affiliated, congregations located there have a smaller pool of people to encourage toward membership. In contrast, areas where *many* people are unaffiliated offer congregations and their worshipers more opportunities for outreach and inviting. While such secularism can reflect a decline in public religious authority, individual beliefs and practices—"private religion"—may still flourish.[10]

Correlations between the affiliated percentage in a county and each of the ten congregational strengths are shown in table 2.2. A correlation is a statistical measure that helps us determine the degree or strength of a relationship. For example, are high rates of affiliation linked to high scores on a congregational strength? A correlation statistic can range between -1 and +1. The closer the correlation statistic is to 1 (either positive or negative) the more the two rates or scores are related. A positive correlation means that as one rate goes up, the other score does as well. A negative correlation means that as one rate goes up, the other score goes down. The closer the correlation statistic is to zero, the more likely it is that the two rates or scores are simply unrelated to each other.

We found that in relatively highly churched areas congregations perform better on four of the ten strengths—Growing Spiritually, Meaningful Worship, Participating in the Congregation, and Caring for Children and Youth (see table 2.2). Congregations in areas with higher percentages of unchurched populations outscore those in churched areas on Focusing on the Community and Welcoming New People. In general, congregations prove to be more vital as the percentage of the churched population rises. Being located in an area where there are many other congregations and many other worshipers should not threaten congregations seeking to be effective or growing numerically. Rather, being in close quarters with other faith communities appears to raise the level of vitality.

Faith group and churched areas: Catholic parishes in highly churched areas maintained the edge in Participating in the Congregation. In less churched areas, Catholic parishes appear to be most successful in Welcoming New People. Mainline Protestant congregations in more highly churched areas reflect a number of strengths. They do well on three of the ten strengths—Growing Spiritually, Meaningful Worship, and Caring for Children and Youth. Finally, conservative Protestant churches reveal a distinctive pattern. These congregations excel in Growing Spiritually, Participating in the Congregation, and Looking to the Future in more highly churched areas.

In general, congregations are less effective in Focusing on the Community as the proportion of the churched population increases. Congregations prove to be less effective in Welcoming New People in highly churched areas as well. However, this is not true for conservative Protestant churches. Conservative Protestant churches attract new worshipers, regardless of the percentage churched in the local area.

Finding Strength in Your Religious Geography

In chapter 5 and the conclusion, we'll return to these issues to compare the influence of highly churched areas and the Bible Belt region to other aspects of congregational location. While congregations cannot relocate to more "favorable" locations in other regions of the United States or in distant counties with more unchurched people, they can discern the unique opportunities for ministry where they are. Larger geographic forces beyond the neighborhood parish are always present. The essential question is, How does our congregation respond to our location's distinct features to build effective ministries?

In *Once upon a Town,* Bob Greene tells how a no-account location made heroes of people willing to see a place's promise.[11] He recounts the real events in a small town, North Platte, Nebraska, that played a memorable role during World War II. During the war, thirty-two trains a day brought troops through the isolated midwestern town on their way to Europe and the Pacific. The trains stopped for only ten minutes. But during the brief stop, soldiers were greeted, fed, given presents, and entertained by the townspeople. Miraculously, by the end of the war the residents of North Platte had touched the lives of *six million* GIs. Neighbors and church groups stayed organized for five straight years, every day from 5:00 a.m. until midnight, to offer kindness to all the men who traveled through North Platte—on their way, perhaps, to die for their country.

The North Platte Canteen closed on April 1, 1946, since most soldiers had returned home by then. The Ladies Aid of St. John's Lutheran Church of Gothenburg comprised most of the volunteers on that final day. Twelve servicemen arrived by train just after the canteen officially closed. Greene describes how the final three volunteers—Mrs. Hutchens, Mrs. T. J. Neid, and Mrs. Traub—had just finished making themselves a pot of coffee. They gave it to the soldiers instead.

While North Platte lies outside the Bible Belt, congregations are plentiful in the area and the county is highly churched.[12] Fortunately, the heroes of this true story didn't ask, "What's a nice congregation like ours doing in a place like this?" Instead, they asked the important question, "What can a nice congregation like ours do in a place like this?"

Discover where your congregation is located.

CHAPTER 3

STRENGTH IN THE COMMUNITY

Many fields, many treasures, many pearls
(One chosen).

G. WAYNE GLICK

How can we accurately describe the places or communities where congregations are located? In previous chapters, we looked at location on a grand scale, defined by regions of the country, states, or counties. In this chapter, we move closer to home to examine location demographically at the community level. These community features portray the context in which each congregation serves—the people and families who live there; their education, employment, and mobility; and the available housing. Can congregations benefit from paying attention to the people in their community?

Researchers often use the U.S. Census—the largest and most reputable source of community data—to depict a specific geographic area. We collected information from the 2000 U.S. Census for a three-mile radius around each participating congregation. This area approximates a circle, six miles across, based on the census tract geography in that location. While we considered a smaller area (a one-mile radius) and a larger area (the county in which the congregation is located) as a statistical base, we found few differences related to the area size when all congregations were considered.[1]

In appendix 6 we list the census information used in our analyses and supply definitions for each demographic trait. While the U.S. Census provides a wealth of statistical data, we selected just those community descriptors most relevant to congregations.

Our research examines a national random sample of congregations, chosen to be representative of all U.S. congregations. Now our focus shifts to the *communities* where these congregations are located. Are the communities around these congregations also representative of communities across the country? Yes! We found that the *communities* where the U.S. Congregational Life Survey (CLS) congregations are located closely mirror the national picture (see table 3.1).

Five Community Types

We clustered census information to identify unique community types. These community types represent the typical communities in which congregations are located. Five meaningful clusters emerged that best distinguish among the communities in which U.S. CLS congregations are located.[2] Our typology groups communities based on their similarities across twenty-six traits. The traits used to develop these community types are present to a greater or lesser degree in all communities. One trait we've examined, for example, is mobility—the percentage of people in the community who have moved in the past five years. Across the country, 46% of Americans moved in that time frame. In our community types, those locations where mobility is high (averaging 68% mobility) form one community type. Communities where mobility is relatively low (averaging 38%) form another community type.

Rural Communities

Everson, Washington, a small town of about two thousand people, sits at the foot of the Cascade Mountains in the northwest corner of the state. Dairy farms, fruit orchards, and berry fields contribute to Everson's economy.

About 1,100 people live in Poseyville, a community in southern Indiana. Most residents are married, white non-Hispanics. The median house value is about $70,000.

COMPARING COMMUNITIES:
PROFILE FOR ALL U.S. COMMUNITIES AND
U.S. CONGREGATIONAL LIFE SURVEY COMMUNITIES

	U.S. Census 2000	U.S. CLS Communities
Population, Housing, and Households		
Living in urban areas	79%	69%
Mobility (moved in past five years)	46%	45%
Minority population	23%	26%
Foreign-born population	11%	6%
Number of households (density)	—	18,756
Average household size	2.59	2.55
Owner-occupied housing	66%	68%
Housing built in past five years	10%	10%
Population growth in past ten years	13%	10%
Families		
Married, children at home	24%	22%
Married, no children at home	28%	28%
Female-headed households	7%	7%
Education		
College degree	24%	20%
Some college, but no degree	27%	27%
No high school degree	20%	21%
Employment and Income		
Average household income	$56,604	$47,126
Working professionals	34%	29%
Working in service or sales	42%	41%
Working in farming or construction	25%	29%
Unemployed	4%	6%
Living in poverty	12%	14%
Age		
Under age 18	26%	25%
Age 18–29	17%	17%
Age 30–44	24%	22%
Age 45–64	22%	22%
Age 65 or older	12%	13%

Table 3.1

In table 3.2 we show the five clusters and summarize the census information that makes each cluster unique. As you read about each cluster, consider which one best describes the community where your congregation is located. While some communities may appear distinctly different from any of these five, careful analysis will reveal which community type fits your congregation's community best.

Rural communities: The first community type, Rural, includes places where a majority live outside urban areas, whether in small towns or rural areas. The smallest percentage of people moved in the past five years in Rural communities (just 38%). Population density is lowest here, too, with fewer than five thousand households in a three-mile radius. Most residents are married and own their own homes. Few have college degrees in these types of communities, and the largest employment sector is farming and construction. Unemployment is low. The age distribution includes relatively few young adults who are between the ages of 18 and 29. One-quarter of participating congregations are located in Rural communities.

Growing Suburban communities: Like Rural communities, the second community type includes primarily traditional families—married couples, many with children living at home. Adults are well-educated, employed in professional and managerial positions,

> ### Growing Suburban Communities
>
> Clear Lake, Texas, in the bay area of Houston (around the Johnson Space Center and the University of Houston), thrives on the aerospace, retail, and tourism industries. Master-planned residential communities are common.
>
> Westborough, Massachusetts, thirty miles from Boston, enjoyed a 27% growth rate between 1990 and 2000. Many residents live there for the excellent schools and commute to white-collar jobs in the city. One-quarter of residents are under the age of 18.

and own their homes rather than rent. Those between the ages of 30 and 64 predominate. Unemployment and poverty rates are low here. Of the five clusters, this one shows the most population growth, the highest household incomes, and the most new homes (built in the past five years). This cluster includes about 21% of participating congregations.

Small Cities and Stable Suburban communities: The third community type, located primarily in smaller cities and the suburbs of

Small Cities and Stable Suburban Communities

Pueblo, in southern Colorado, with an average household size of 2.4 people, struggles with the decline of its major industry—steel. The city has experienced little growth in recent years.

Many older adults live in the northern suburbs of Knoxville, Tennessee (18% are 65 or older), and few homes there are new (only 3% were built in the past five years). Only 20% of residents are under the age of 18. Few minorities call this area home.

Economically Distressed Urban Communities

Midway Airport in Chicago, Illinois, is situated in an urban area. Three in ten residents in the local community lack a high school diploma. Only 1% of homes were built between 1990 and 2000.

In downtown Los Angeles, most people living in the neighborhoods around the University of Southern California and the Coliseum are minorities (primarily Hispanic). Income falls below $15,000 for 41% of households. The area's population base is declining.

larger cities, has the highest percentage of older people—16% are age 65 or older. Population growth is almost nonexistent in these communities, and few immigrants live here. Among the five types, this one has a particularly low percentage of homes built in the previous five years (6%). About 28% of participating congregations can be found in this Small Cities and Stable Suburban community type.

Economically Distressed Urban communities: The last two community types reflect urban areas of the country where population density (number of households) is relatively high. The population in Economically Distressed Urban communities experiences high rates of unemployment and poverty and low rates of homeownership. Many people have not graduated from high school, and female-headed households are more numerous. Despite having virtually no population growth, these communities have lots of children. In addition, of the five community types, people in this cluster are most likely to be of a minority racial-ethnic background. Economically Distressed Urban communities encompass two in ten congregations.

High-Mobility Urban communities: In the remaining community type, as in Economically Distressed Urban communities, relatively few people are married. Many well-educated singles rent their apartments or houses, and population mobility is high—64% moved within the past five years. Of the five clusters, this one has the lowest proportion of children under age 18— just 17%. However, this type has the highest percentage of people between the ages of 18 and 29. Such communities have the highest population density (the number of households in a three-mile radius). The fewest congregations overall fall in High-Mobility Urban communities (only 10%).

High-Mobility Urban Communities

Three-quarters of the residents of Ann Arbor, Michigan, home to the University of Michigan, hold college degrees, and about 12% are foreign-born. As in many college towns, most people are never-married singles (about two-thirds) and many live in rental units (apartments, duplexes, etc.).

Alexandria, Virginia, just outside the nation's capital, is home to many professionals working in government, the military, or private firms that support the government. Six in ten residents moved in the past five years, and two-thirds are college graduates.

Strengths of Congregations Located in Each Community Type

These community types help us challenge many long-standing assumptions about whether location

FIVE COMMUNITY TYPES

	Rural	Growing Suburban	Small Cities and Stable Suburban	Economically Distressed Urban	High-Mobility Urban
Population, Housing, and Households					
Living in urban areas	27%	**89%**	**86%**	**98%**	**94%**
Mobility (moved in past five years)	38%	46%	45%	46%	**64%**
Minority population	12%	20%	17%	**58%**	**32%**
Foreign-born population	2%	**11%**	4%	7%	**12%**
Number of households (density)	4,207	19,199	13,630	**28,176**	**55,626**
Average household size	**2.62**	**2.63**	2.37	**2.64**	2.24
Owner-occupied housing	**80%**	**75%**	64%	56%	40%
Housing built in past five years	**14%**	**16%**	6%	5%	10%
Population growth in past ten years	14%	**26%**	2%	1%	15%
Families					
Married, children at home	**26%**	**28%**	20%	18%	14%
Married, no children at home	**34%**	**32%**	28%	21%	19%
Female-headed households	5%	5%	8%	**12%**	5%
Education					
College degree	13%	**36%**	20%	16%	**40%**
Some college, but no degree	25%	**29%**	28%	28%	27%
No high school degree	22%	10%	19%	**27%**	14%
Employment and Income					
Average household income	$44,841	**$72,412**	$44,065	$40,091	$50,370
Working professionals	25%	**42%**	30%	26%	**39%**
Working in service or sales	36%	40%	43%	**46%**	45%
Working in farming or construction	**37%**	18%	26%	28%	16%
Unemployed	4%	3%	6%	**9%**	8%
Living in poverty	10%	5%	13%	**21%**	**21%**
Age					
Under age 18	26%	25%	24%	**28%**	17%
Age 18–29	13%	13%	16%	19%	**38%**
Age 30–44	23%	**24%**	22%	22%	20%
Age 45–64	24%	**24%**	22%	20%	16%
Age 65 or older	13%	13%	**16%**	12%	9%

Note: All values in the table are (weighted) means. Bold numbers: This community type scores higher on this trait (all differences are statistically significant at the $p < .05$ level).

Table 3.2

MYTH TRAP

As communities gain new residents, local congregations automatically gain new worshipers.

One in three worshipers in the typical congregation is new (began attending there in the past five years). But in the average community nearly *one in two* people (44%) is new (moved there in the past five years).

Do congregations benefit from many new community residents? The answer is more often yes for mainline and conservative Protestant churches and more often no for Catholic parishes. As the percentage of new community residents increases, the number of new worshipers in mainline and conservative Protestant congregations also increases. In the typical Catholic parish an increase in community newcomers less often translates to increasing numbers of new worshipers.

But the answer also varies from congregation to congregation. Even in communities with many new residents, some congregations fail to add new worshipers. What is your congregation doing to identify and attract your community's newcomers?

determines congregational vitality. For example, can congregations located in Economically Distressed Urban communities be effective? Do congregations located in Rural communities face more difficulties in doing ministry? Do congregations in Growing Suburban communities attract more new members? Do congregations in different types of locations show different strengths? In other words, how closely linked is community type and congregational effectiveness?

Congregations located in each of the five community types demonstrate above-average scores on at least one strength. In each column, at least one score in bold reveals where these congregations tend to excel. This is good news for all congregations. *Regardless of congregational location*, effective ministry can happen.

Equally important, the findings shown in table 3.3 confirm that the *pattern of strengths* differs substantially among the community types. Strengths typical of congregations in Rural communities are different from the strengths of congregations in Economically Distressed Urban communities.

Ten congregational strengths and the average score for congregations within each community type are shown in table 3.3. Like the previous tables, bold scores show areas where congregations in that community type excel. Again, the scores in this table represent averages across all congregations in each community type.[3]

Strengths of congregations in Rural communities: Congregations in Rural areas can claim many strengths. They do particularly well in helping worshipers grow spiritually, providing meaningful worship, involving many worshipers, building a strong sense of belonging among members, caring for children and youth, helping worshipers share their faith with others, and empowering their worshipers. Small congregations with fewer than one hundred in worship, which predominate in Rural areas, also claim many of these same strengths.[4] One characteristic presents a challenge to congregations in Rural communities: Focusing on the Community.

Strengths of congregations in Growing Suburban communities: Congregations in these types of communities, where many families have children at home, excel in Caring for Children and Youth. Such congregations also stand out in their community involvement (Focusing on the Community). This may be related to the higher average incomes, higher educational levels, and employment in professional and managerial professions in such communities. Welcoming New People (those who have been attending for five years or less) also stands out as a strength of congregations in growing suburbs—likely linked to the increasing population in these areas. At the same time, congregations in Growing Suburban communities also face challenges in facilitating spiritual growth, involving worshipers in congregational activities, ensuring that those who attend feel they belong there, and helping worshipers share their faith with others.

Strengths of congregations in Small Cities and Stable Suburban communities:

Congregations in these areas, like those in Growing Suburban communities, excel in nurturing children and youth and involvement in the local community. Yet the linkages here are different. Small Cities and Stable Suburban communities include many residents age 65 or older who are less likely to be in the labor force. Worshipers who are retired and finished rearing children have the time to give to community service activities. In six other areas, congregations in these types of communities have considerable room for improvement. Several of these are the same areas of challenge confronting congregations in Growing Suburban communities: Growing Spiritually, Meaningful Worship, Participating in the Congregation, Sense of Belonging, Sharing Faith, and Empowering Leadership.

Strengths of congregations in Economically Distressed Urban communities: Urban communities that are economically disadvantaged must cope with several challenges. Nonetheless, congregations in these communities excel in three areas: worshipers find the services to be meaningful, they are comfortable sharing their faith with others, and they believe their congregations value the gifts and services of all members. Despite having the largest percentage of children under age 18, scores on Caring for Children and Youth do not measure up to those of congregations in other community types. The scarce resources available in these communities may limit the programming and services offered for young people. Congregations in economically stressed communities score somewhat lower than congregations located elsewhere on Focusing on the Community. Such congregations may find that assisting members requires almost all available resources, leaving little for those outside their doors. The final challenge of congregations in these communities lies in attracting and retaining new people. With near-zero population growth, these congregations do not enjoy an ongoing supply of new neighbors who might be potential new members, yet they can warmly welcome area residents who attend their services for the first time.

Strengths of congregations in High-Mobility Urban communities: Congregations located in areas with many young, educated singles face many challenges. Their strength lies in community involvement. Above-average incomes and few child-rearing responsibilities frees people in these congregations to focus on the needs of others. Yet congregations in these types of communities score lower than other congregations do on seven of the ten strengths. Congregations in High-Mobility Urban communities face challenges on these strengths: Growing Spiritually, Meaningful Worship, Participating in the Congregation, Sense of Belonging, and Sharing Faith. Many people in these communities are between the ages of 18 and 29 and are likely to be recent college graduates. As such, their focus may be on establishing careers and building relationships. This focus often takes priority over establishing congregational connections at that stage in life. Congregations in these types of locations also score somewhat lower on Caring for Children and Youth and Empowering Leadership.

STRENGTHS OF CONGREGATIONS LOCATED IN EACH COMMUNITY TYPE

	Rural	Growing Suburban	Small Cities and Stable Suburban	Economically Distressed Urban	High-Mobility Urban	Overall
1 Growing Spiritually	**51**	44	45	49	38	48
2 Meaningful Worship	**65**	61	60	**66**	52	62
3 Participating in the Congregation	**65**	56	57	62	49	60
4 Sense of Belonging	**40**	34	34	36	30	36
5 Caring for Children and Youth	**53**	**52**	**52**	45	46	50
6 Focusing on the Community	31	**36**	**36**	28	**39**	33
7 Sharing Faith	**37**	28	26	**37**	21	32
8 Welcoming New People	33	**42**	33	31	32	33
9 Empowering Leadership	**52**	49	46	**53**	39	49
10 Looking to the Future	41	43	40	41	37	41
Overall Vitality (average of all ten)	**45**	44	43	44	38	44

Note: All values in the table are (weighted) means. Bold numbers: Congregations in this community type score higher than average on this strength (a statistically significant difference at the p < .05 level).

Table 3.3

Community Type and Region

Where are these community types located? Does the region in which your congregation is located determine your community type? No. Congregations in *all five community types* surface in *every* region of the country—Northeast, Midwest, South, and West. Congregations in all five community types exist both in the Bible Belt and in areas outside the Bible Belt. Congregations in all five community types turn up in red states that traditionally support Republican candidates and blue states that typically support Democratic candidates. (How the five community types are spread out across the regions is shown in appendix 7.)

Faith Groups and Community Types

What explains the tendency of congregations in Rural communities to develop more strengths than congregations in other communities? Part of the explanation lies with the geographic concentration of congregations affiliated with a particular faith group (see chapters 1 and 2).

   In table 3.4 we present the faith group distribution of congregations within each community type. Congregations of all faith groups exist in each community type. Catholic churches are more common in three community types: Small Cities and Stable Suburban, Economically Distressed Urban, and High-Mobility Urban communities. Rural communities and Growing Suburban communities claim very few Catholic churches. Mainline Protestant churches are more common in three community types— both suburban types (Growing and Stable) and in High-Mobility Urban communities— and less common in Rural and Economically Distressed Urban communities. Conservative Protestant churches more typically populate Rural communities and Economically Distressed Urban areas.

   Other factors also contribute to the many strengths of congregations in Rural communities. These include the fact that such community types emerge more often in the South, a region where many congregational strengths appear.[5]

WHAT TYPES OF CONGREGATIONS
ARE FOUND IN EACH COMMUNITY TYPE?

	Rural	Growing Suburban	Small Cities and Stable Suburban	Economically Distressed Urban	High-Mobility Urban	Overall
Catholic	3%	9%	**17%**	**19%**	**21%**	12%
Mainline Protestant	38%	**56%**	**47%**	23%	**48%**	40%
Conservative Protestant	**59%**	36%	36%	**58%**	30%	49%

Bold number: This faith group is more common in this type of community.

Table 3.4

Finding Strength in Any Community

These results show that congregations can go beyond the ordinary in any location. Congregations show signs of strength in all types of communities. Congregational leaders and worshipers cannot blame their location for lackluster ministry. These findings offer a challenge to all congregations to: (a) identify and build on their strengths, and (b) celebrate the unique location that is theirs and theirs alone. What makes your congregation's location unique? How can your location become a strength?

The story of a far-from-ordinary congregation illustrates the point. Valley Open Bible Fellowship's niche is food. The church, located in Big Lake, Alaska, knows that many of its area's three thousand households are living without the basics—electricity, running water, and food. So every week the church of forty to fifty regular attendees provides a full-course meal from its 9-foot x 10-foot kitchen for some sixty unchurched people.[6] Instead of using an economically distressed location as an excuse for ignoring those outside its doors, this church made the community's needs the core of its local mission. This small church recognized its unique location, embraced the people outside its doors, and made location one of its strengths. Your congregation can do the same.

Apply the good match principle.

CHAPTER 4

Strength in a Perfect Match

In all affairs, it's a healthy thing now and then
to hang a question mark on the things you have long taken for granted.

BERTRAND RUSSELL

We give Scandinavians credit for observing, "There is no bad weather, just bad clothes." This simple insight about the importance of a good match between the local weather and appropriate clothing is worth repeating. Congregations can also carefully consider the match between "who they are" and the local "outside temperature"—the community context in which they worship and serve. Is it a good match? Does the profile of the congregation match the local community's profile? Would a closer demographic match between congregation and community result in more effectiveness in the congregation's various ministries?

The Good Match Principle

Contingency theory first explored how an organization adapts to its environment and whether that adaptation might relate to organizational success.[1] Some of the principles of contingency theory can be applied to congregations as well. Many believe that congregations whose internal features and approach are a "good match" with the community achieve the most effective ministry outcomes. They argue that if a congregation's adopted strategies are not consistent with the local context, the strategies fail.[2] But is the "good match" principle true?

Why might a match be important? Two central concepts of contingency theory are effectiveness and efficiency. In the theory's framework, a congregation is effective "when it realizes its purposes and accomplishes its goals."[3] A congregation achieves efficiency when it uses the least amount of resources to accomplish its purposes and goals. According to contingency theory, a good match maximizes effectiveness and efficiency.

Does a match between congregation and community matter? To answer this question, we compared each congregation with its local community profile on fifteen demographic traits involving the population categories of race and immigration, education, income, age, and family type. Each demographic trait is measured for the congregation based on worshipers' survey responses—how they describe themselves. The community traits describe people living in a three-mile radius around the congregation based on U.S. Census information (as was used in chapter 3). For each demographic trait, we determined how well congregations match their communities.

What is a match? We measure a "match" by looking at the difference between the congregation's percentage on a demographic trait and the community's percentage on the same trait. For example, if 30% of a congregation's worshipers have a college degree, but only 10% of the community residents have a college degree, the difference between the two is 20 percentage points. Throughout this chapter, we designate differences of 10 percentage points or less as a "match" and those that exceed 10 percentage points as a "mismatch." The match or mismatch is based on the absolute difference between the two scores—either the congregation or the community score can be up to ten percentage points higher and still be considered a match. We then look at the pattern of matches or mismatches for each trait across all U.S. Congregational Life Survey congregations.[4]

A perfect match? Congregations match their communities closely on some dimensions but not others. (See figure 4.1 for a summary of what percentages of U.S. CLS congregations demographically match their respective communities.) Congregations are least likely to match their surrounding community when it comes to one important age range—the percentages of people in the congregation and community who are between the ages of 18 and 44. This age group roughly represents the post–baby boomer generations—generations X and Y—whose religious behavior will impact current and future congregational life. In only 15% of all congregations does the current percentage of worshipers in that age range match (within 10 percentage points) the percentage in the community.

On the other hand, the majority of congregations (62%) match their community when it comes to the percentage of people in middle- and high-income brackets. Congregations mirror the community's economic makeup better than they reflect their community's age profile. Congregations often reflect the community in terms of the percentage of residents who are unemployed (95% match their local community) or foreign-born (88% match their local community).

What are the closest community-congregation matches? At least six in ten congregations match their community profile on four demographic traits—high-income households, middle-income households, foreign-born residents, and unemployed adults.

What are the biggest community-congregation mismatches? No more than four in ten congregations match their community percentages on three demographic traits, all related to age: adults 18 to 44 years of age, 18 to 29 years of age, and 65 years of age and older.

Important Findings

When we compared the composition of local communities to the demographic characteristics of worshipers, several differences emerged:

- Communities tend to be *more* racially diverse than the worshipers in the congregations located there.

- Only a few congregations function as immigrant enclaves—where the majority of worshipers are immigrants in a community where few are immigrants (about 2%).

WHAT PERCENTAGE OF CONGREGATIONS MATCH THEIR COMMUNITIES?

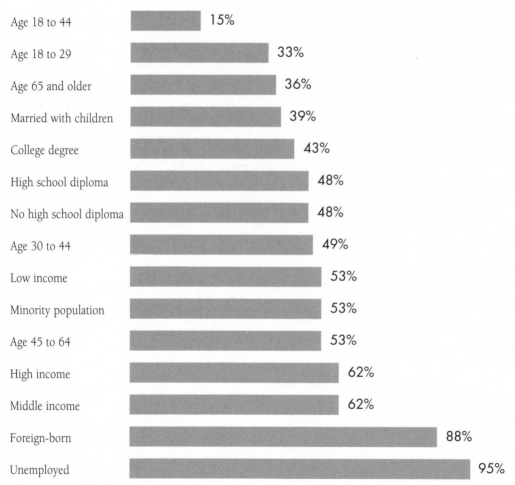

Age 18 to 44	15%
Age 18 to 29	33%
Age 65 and older	36%
Married with children	39%
College degree	43%
High school diploma	48%
No high school diploma	48%
Age 30 to 44	49%
Low income	53%
Minority population	53%
Age 45 to 64	53%
High income	62%
Middle income	62%
Foreign-born	88%
Unemployed	95%

How to read this table: 15% of the surveyed congregations had about the same percentage of people age 18 to 44 as their surrounding community. The rest (85%) did not match their community on this important demographic. In 39% of the congregations, there was about the same percentage of traditional families (married with children at home) as in the surrounding community. The remaining 61% of congregations did not match their community's family profile.

Figure 4.1

- Many congregations draw a larger percentage of traditional families (married couples with children living at home) than expected, given their community's demographic profile.

- Typically, a higher percentage of young adults (between 18 and 29 years old) resides in the community than are attracted to congregations. Thus, young adult worshipers are vastly underrepresented in congregational life.

- Congregations typically attract more worshipers in the 45 to 64 years of age group than expected, given the community profile.

- Most congregations have a much higher percentage of older worshipers (65 years of age and older) than the percentage of older people who live in the community.

- Compared to their communities, congregations tend to have more people with at least a college degree.

The Big Picture

We presented a picture of how all congregations—regardless of faith group—match or mismatch their community's profile. If we reproduced the previous figure, looking at each faith group—Catholic, mainline Protestant, and conservative Protestant—would the patterns be the same? In most ways, yes. But for several traits where we've compared the congregation and community—adults 65 years of age and older, adults 18 to 44 years of age, traditional families, and high school graduates—we found important faith group differences. In this section, we compare how faith groups differ in their congregation-community matches on these four traits. Because the congregation-community match for those between 18 and 44 years of age showed the most powerful statistical relationships to the ten congregational strengths, we examine these patterns in depth. Again, we explore faith group differences for this match outcome.

Faith Families and Their Community-Congregation Match

In figure 4.2 we show where congregations in the three faith traditions diverge *most* in their community-congregation matches. The matches include two aspects of the age distribution, two views of the educational level, and family composition.

All types of congregations attract more people 65 and older, but mainline Protestant churches do so more than others. Over 40% of conservative Protestant churches and Catholic parishes, but only 24% of mainline Protestants, match their community profile for residents 65 and older. In all three faith groups, congregations that do not match their communities on this factor tend to have *more* older worshipers than are in their communities. Among mainline Protestant churches, this is even more pronounced, resulting in even fewer such congregations matching their communities on this trait.

Conservative Protestant churches attract more 18- to 44-year-olds. Compared to congregations in other faith groups, conservative Protestant churches draw more people 18 to 44 years of age. Thus, their congregation-community match rate (26%) is much higher than the 18-to-44 age-group match rates for the other two groups (4% for Catholic parishes and 6% for mainline Protestants). This match on 18- to 44-year-olds is the greatest difference between the three faith groups. Nonetheless, in all three groups, congregations have fewer worshipers in this age range than would be expected, given the many community residents in that age bracket.

All types of congregations attract more traditional families, but conservative Protestant churches do so the most. Another area where faith traditions influence the congregation-community match is on the traditional-family demographic. Catholic parishes and mainline Protestant churches match their community profile equally often when it comes to married couples with children at home—about 45% of such churches show a match. Conservative Protestant churches have lower match rates (32% overall) because they attract even *more* families with children than would be expected given their community profile.

All types of congregations attract more high school graduates (without any college education), but conservative Protestant churches do so the most. All faith groups attract a higher percentage of people whose highest level of education is a high school degree than the percentage in their communities. Similar proportions of Catholic parishes and mainline Protestant churches match their communities on the percentage of worshipers and residents whose highest degree is a high school diploma (54% and 58% match, respectively). However, conservative Protestant churches have lower match rates for adults with a high school education (only 38% of such churches show a match) because these churches attract even *more* high school graduates than expected given the percentage in the community.

> Compared to congregations, *local communities* have more:
> Young adults, 18 to 44 years old
> Residents without high school diplomas
> Members of racial or ethnic groups
> High-income families

All types of congregations attract more worshipers with college or more advanced degrees; this is particularly true for mainline Protestant churches. In all three faith groups, the percentage of worshipers who hold college or more advanced degrees surpasses the percentage in the local community. About half of Catholic parishes (52%) and conservative Protestant congregations (48%) match their communities on this trait. Only about a third of mainline Protestant congregations (35%) do so because such churches attract even more college or advanced degree graduates than expected given the educational levels in the local community.

> Compared to local communities, *congregations* have more:
> Worshipers with a college degree or more education
> Adults, 65 years of age or older
> Traditional families—married couples with children at home

Testing the Good Match Principle

What impact does a match or mismatch between the characteristics of worshipers and the characteristics of community members have on congregational strengths? Does congregational

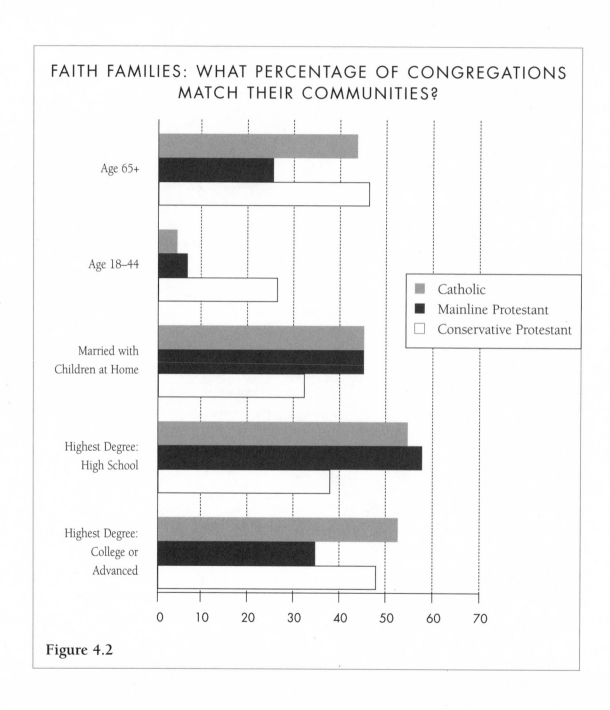

FAITH FAMILIES: WHAT PERCENTAGE OF CONGREGATIONS MATCH THEIR COMMUNITIES?

Figure 4.2

vitality soar or suffer when worshipers differ substantially from those in the community?

Congregational strength results when congregations match the community's percentage on adults age 18 to 44. We found the demographic match on the 18- to 44-year-old age group to be most closely related to congregational strength. This match yields the most dramatic results for congregational ministry. A close match between the congregation and the community on the percentage of adults who are in the 18- to 44-year-old age group makes for greater congregational strength in eight out of ten strengths—Growing Spiritually, Meaningful Worship, Sense of Belonging, Caring for Children and Youth, Sharing Faith, Welcoming New People, Empowering Leadership, and Looking to the Future. For example, congregations that match their community's percentage of adults in the 18- to 44-year-old age group invest in children and youth ministries. A close 18- to 44-year-old match between congregation and community is also significantly related to the strength of Welcoming New People. Finally, congregations that closely mirror the 18- to 44-year-old community profile also exhibit the strength of Looking to the Future.

Congregations attracting a percentage of people 18 to 44 years old comparable to that in their community also score above average on the Overall Vitality Index. The 18- to 44-year-old age demographic is key to developing a sustainable, effective ministry. This age group often includes many young parents who bring their children when they attend services or participate in congregational activities.

However, the 18- to 44-year-old congregation-community *mismatch* is linked to one congregational strength—Focusing on the Community. When congregations don't look like their community on this factor (fewer 18- to 44-year-olds), their worshipers tend to do *more* advocacy and social service activities in their community. This seemingly contrary finding may stem from having many older adult worshipers who have more leisure time and spend some of that time caring for others in the community. A higher percentage of older adult worshipers drives up congregational efforts to make a difference in the community.

Just because many current congregations have the pattern of strength in Focusing on the Community and fewer 18- to 44-year-olds does not dictate what the future holds.

Myth Trap

As the largest age group in this country, young children are the greatest source of future members.

Flawed fact: In 1900—and even as late as 1950—children five years of age and younger numbered more than any other five-year slice of the U.S. population. But due to declining birthrates and increasing age spans, that is no longer the case. In 2000, people age 35 to 39 (born at the end of the baby boom between 1960 and 1964) outnumbered those in every other age group.

Household size also decreased during the century. In 1900, high birthrates and the prevalence of extended families in the home resulted in large households—many with more than seven people. In 2000, the majority of households (58%) consisted of just one or two people.

Because children become future members, declining birthrates and smaller households contribute to declining membership. Fewer children mean congregations must think differently about their ministry and growth strategies. No longer can they rely on an abundant supply of future new members among the children of their current members.

Flawed logic: Even before the decline of birthrates and household sizes, children were not the main focus of congregations hoping to grow larger. Parents select the congregation that families attend—not young children. If anything, *young parents* are the greatest source of future members.

Yet, many people drop out of congregational life in early adulthood and decide to return when they are themselves young parents. When it's their turn to choose a congregation they often select one that ministers effectively with small children *and* young parents. Quality programs for youth are but one part of the pie—congregations must consider all ages!

Congregations with many young worshipers could (and some do) have a ministry focus that includes a commitment to community ministry. Likewise, a congregation could (and some do) build on their Focusing on the Community strength by incorporating larger numbers of young worshipers.

A Close Match and Faith Family

When it comes to adults age 18 to 44 years of age, does the "good match principle" hold for congregations in all three faith groups?

Matching the community on adults age 18 to 44 creates the biggest yield for conservative Protestant churches. A close congregation-community match on the percentages of people between 18 and 44 years old holds little importance for Catholic parish vitality and moderate importance for mainline Protestant vitality. However, a close congregation-community match yields big returns for conservative Protestant churches. Catholic parishes that match their surrounding community's 18- to 44-year-old age demographic show more strength on Welcoming New People. Both mainline Protestant and conservative Protestant churches show similar strength when they match the same age demographic. Mainline Protestant churches that match their community's percentage of people in the 18- to 44-year-old age range flourish in one additional strength area—Looking to the Future.[5]

Conservative Protestant churches show the greatest sensitivity to this match factor. When these churches closely mirror the percentage of 18- to 44-year-olds in the community, they achieve greater strength in a number of areas. Their close match yields strength in Caring for Children and Youth, Welcoming New People, and Looking to the Future.

However, when the percentage of 18- to 44-year-olds in the community exceeds the percentage in conservative Protestant churches, these congregations seem to benefit in several ways from the mismatch. Such churches achieve greater ministry strength when they look *less* like the community for this age group on two of the ten strengths: Participating in the Congregation and Sharing Faith.

Finding Strength in a Community Match

In 1972, Dean Kelley published his controversial book, *Why Conservative Churches Are Growing*. He argued that theologically conservative churches grew because they made "strict" demands on their members. In contrast, liberal churches were declining because they made few demands on their members and tolerated more than one point of view. His charge that "the churches are dying today not because they are merely religious, but because they are not very religious at all" incited some leaders. But his arguments were more complex and nuanced than his book title suggested. Kelley later said he should have titled his book, "Why Conservative Churches Are Strong."[6]

More than thirty years later leaders still argue about what makes churches strong. Identifying a single factor as the *one* reason for strength or growth leads nowhere because congregations are complex organizations. However, congregations that match their community on an important demographic group—residents 18 to 44 years of age—grasp a powerful facet for successful ministry. Attracting worshipers in this age range says that their mission, programs, and leadership are in tune with the community's future—and the congregation's future.

Identify what supports church growth.

CHAPTER 5

MULTIPLE SOURCES OF GEOGRAPHIC STRENGTH

When perception and reality duel, perception usually wins.

HERB MILLER

In previous chapters we've reviewed the ways a congregation's location might relate to its vitality. We began with the largest geographic category—U.S. Census regions—and moved to increasingly smaller geographic areas—red-state/blue-state differences, the Bible Belt distinction, the county's religious affiliation rate, the community type, and the match between a congregation's worshipers and the people in the local community. Each geographic level offered one view of location's possible impact on congregational life.

Yet we made no attempt to compare the relative weight of these different location factors. Further, we didn't control for other nonlocation factors that also contribute to congregational vitality or compare their relative importance. Typically our puzzling over cause and effect considers the relationship between only two factors. For example, when we eat too much, we gain weight. But we know that fully understanding weight gain and other issues in our lives requires examining multiple factors. Weight gain is not only related to how much we eat, but *what* we eat. But even that is not enough. Exercise, metabolism rates, disease, age, heredity, and other elements all play a role in weight gain and loss. And other issues come into play. One factor—for example, lack of exercise—may contribute more to weight gain for some people, while another factor—perhaps heredity—plays a more important role for others. Ignoring these complexities means we miss the full picture.

We face a similar challenge as we seek to fully understand congregational vitality. In this chapter we attempt to bring the various threads from previous chapters together to look at the relative impact of these multiple aspects of location on congregational vitality. In addition, we take up the question of how location—in its many facets—and congregational strengths contribute to numerical membership growth.

We do not believe that numerical growth is the only indicator of congregational health. Increasing the number of visitors and members is but one of many ways to assess organizational well-being. Some congregations believe that increasing worship attendance and adding members is what God requires as a top priority. But others place greater emphasis on caring for current attendees, community outreach, or outstanding worship as their primary expressions of faithfulness. Our research indicates congregations need multiple strengths to be effective.

We acknowledge that numerical growth is not irrelevant. Congregations cannot ignore changes in their membership or worship attendance. Without turning around a continual decline in worship attendance, congregations experiencing such changes will face reductions in staff or programs, and finally, extinction. Likewise congregations facing continual increases in membership cannot ignore the implications of that change. Without gearing up to accommodate an increase in attendance, the increase is not likely to be sustained.

In earlier chapters, we examined the impact of location on ten measures of congregational strength and an overall vitality measure (an average across the ten strength measures). Now we consider how well location predicts congregational vitality (using the overall vitality measure), and how well location *and* congregational vitality together predict congregational growth. Because congregations in different faith traditions often use different criteria to determine membership, we use average worship attendance as the measure of a congregation's size. Our measure of numerical growth (or decline) is the percentage change in average worship attendance in the previous five years.

We know from previous research (our own and that of other scholars) that a number of factors influence congregational vitality and growth. To determine the influence of location on vitality and growth, we included a range of other congregational features in our analyses. Several of these factors describe the people who worship in the congregation: their average age and income, the percentage who are female, and the percentage of college graduates. Other factors we've included describe the congregation: its size, the number of years the congregation has been holding services at its current location, the faith group the congregation is part of, and its numerical growth (the percentage increase or decrease in average worship attendance).

What Factors Predict Congregational Vitality?

When we analyzed the role that worshiper demographics, congregational features, and location played in increasing overall vitality, a consistent picture emerged. *By and large, congregational location plays a minimal role in the strength that congregations can claim.* Of the many features we studied, just three factors are related to greater congregational vitality: the faith group of a congregation, the congregation's numerical growth in the previous five

What is related to *greater* congregational vitality?

Congregational Features
- Faith family—conservative Protestant church
- Numerical growth (increasing worship attendance)

Location Factors
- 18- to 44-year-old congregation-community match

> ## What is related to *less* congregational vitality?
>
> Worshiper Demographics
> - Higher percentage of college-educated worshipers
>
> Location Factors
> - High-Mobility Urban communities
> - Western region of the United States
> - More years at current location

years, and whether the percentage of worshipers who are aged 18 to 44 years matches the 18- to 44-year-old percentage in the local community.

The fact that faith group is related to greater congregational vitality confirms previous results.[1] We know that, on average, conservative Protestant churches score higher on eight of the ten strengths. These results make obvious that even after taking into account the impact of other factors (many measures of location plus congregational age and worshipers' age, education, and income), faith group remains important.

The second factor that helps to predict congregational vitality is numerical growth. Congregations that have experienced more growth in recent years are more likely to be strong congregations. As the next section demonstrates, congregational strengths also predict numerical growth. Numerically growing congregations possess many strengths, *and* strong congregations also tend to add new members.

Finally, the single location factor (out of the twelve location factors we studied) that contributes to congregational strength is the match between the congregation and community on those aged 18 to 44. This underscores the importance of incorporating young adults and indicates that congregations that focus on attracting worshipers in that age range build vitality.

Our analyses revealed that four factors actually predict *less* congregational vitality. In other words, congregations with high scores on these measures proved to be less vital congregations overall. First, congregations with more college-educated worshipers exhibit lower vitality. Then, three location factors predict less vitality: being located in the current location for many years; being located in High-Mobility Urban areas where many young, well-educated singles live; and being located in the country's western region, where religion is less dominant.

One of these four factors producing less vitality operates independently of location: worshipers' education. Congregations with many well-educated worshipers find challenges in becoming high-vitality communities of faith. Of the three faith groups, mainline

What is *not* related to congregational vitality?

Worshiper Demographics
- Percentage of female worshipers
- Average age of worshipers
- Average income of worshipers

Congregational Features
- Size of congregation (average worship attendance)

Location Factors
- Red or blue state
- Red or blue county
- Bible Belt
- Percentage of churched population in the county
- Rural communities
- Growing Suburban communities
- Small Cities and Stable Suburban communities
- Economically Distressed Urban communities

Protestant congregations attract worshipers with the highest average educational levels, and these congregations tend to score lower than conservative Protestant congregations on many of the ten strengths.

The many other features we inspected—including most of the location factors—have *no* relationship to congregational vitality. Worshiper demographics (age, income, and gender), congregational size, and eight measures of location are not related to congregational vitality. Most of the location factors we examined do not play a role in congregational strength. These findings suggest that *location fails as a major predictor of vitality*. Congregations in all locations can be strong and effective.

What Factors Predict Congregational Growth?

We then looked at the ability of worshiper demographics, congregational features, location, and congregational vitality to predict numerical growth. In these analyses, we use the congregation's scores on each of the ten strengths separately as potential predictors of growth, rather than using the overall vitality measure. This allows us to examine the relative contribution of each strength to numerical growth.

What is related to numerical growth?

Emphasis on These Congregational Strengths
- Welcoming New People
- Meaningful Worship
- Participating in the Congregation
- Caring for Children and Youth
- Sense of Belonging

Location Factors
- More years at current location

What is related to numerical decline?

Emphasis on These Congregational Strengths
- Sharing Faith
- Growing Spiritually
- Focusing on the Community

Worshiper Demographics
- Higher percentage of older worshipers
- Higher percentage of college-educated worshipers

Location Factors
- Rural communities

What do our analyses show? *By and large, congregational location plays a minimal role in the numerical growth that congregations experience.* None of our location measures help identify congregations that excel in numerical growth. Instead, we found that many congregational strengths produce numerical growth. Congregations that tend to be growing congregations score high on five of the strengths: Welcoming New People, Meaningful Worship, Participating in the Congregation, Caring for Children and Youth, and providing a Sense of Belonging. In addition, congregations that have been in their current location for many years are more likely to be *growing* churches.[2]

Other factors are related to a *lack* of numerical growth. Congregations with considerable strength in Sharing Faith, Growing Spiritually, and Focusing on the Community are less likely to be growing churches. Similarly, those with large percentages of older worshipers and college-educated worshipers, and congregations located in Rural areas are less likely to be growing.

Congregations scoring high on Growing Spiritually may focus on the spiritual needs of current members and risk neglecting the needs of newcomers. Similarly, congregations

What is *not* related to numerical growth?

Emphasis on These Congregational Strengths
- Empowering Leadership
- Looking to the Future

Worshiper Demographics
- Percentage of female worshipers
- Average income of worshipers

Congregational Features
- Size of congregation (average worship attendance)
- Faith family (Catholic, mainline Protestant, conservative Protestant)

Location Factors
- Region (Northeast, Midwest, South, West)
- Red or blue state
- Red or blue county
- Bible Belt
- Percentage of churched population in the county
- Growing Suburban communities
- Small Cities and Stable Suburban communities
- Economically Distressed Urban communities
- High-Mobility Urban communities
- 18- to 44-year-old congregation-community match

scoring high on Focusing on the Community place considerable emphasis on serving the needs of those outside the congregation. They may de-emphasize or overlook the importance of inviting people to become part of the congregation and welcoming them warmly when they visit. Finally, congregations scoring high on Sharing Faith issue invitations to worship and share their faith with others, but may fail to ensure that their services address potential newcomers' spiritual needs.

The last two factors that contribute to a lack of numerical growth (older worshipers and a rural location) go hand in hand. Congregations in rural areas have fewer young adults than those located elsewhere. Yet we don't want to overemphasize the negative impact of a rural location. The majority of participating rural congregations (57%) experienced growth in the five years before the survey, but their rate of growth was lower than among nonrural congregations.

The remaining factors (two strengths, two measures of worshiper demographics, two congregational features, and ten measures of location) are *not* related to numerical growth. These findings suggest that many beliefs about the power of location are simply myths. Congregations are growing and can grow in all locations.

What Do These Results Say?

First, they point to the relative *un*importance of location in predicting either congregational strength or numerical growth. Despite looking at location in a wide variety of ways, few of our measures of location had an impact on strength or growth. Congregations that are not growing or lack vitality need to look beyond a less-than-ideal location as the cause behind their challenges.

Second, one location factor that does play a role in congregational vitality is the match between a congregation's worshipers and the people in the community who are between 18 and 44 years of age. This critical age group must be recruited and openly welcomed in our congregations, and we need to ensure our worship and activities meet their needs.

Third, a congregation's faith group (whether it is Catholic, conservative Protestant, or mainline Protestant) has considerable power over strength and vitality. Conservative Protestant churches have strengths that surpass those of mainline Protestant churches and Catholic parishes. Here we see that even after we take into account many other congregational characteristics (gender, age, income, education, location), faith group continues to make a difference.

Fourth, these findings suggest that congregational strengths play a central role in determining numerical growth. In contrast to prior church growth research that relied on input from key leaders in congregations, these strengths are measured based on the input of all worshipers in the congregation. Better measurement equals greater clarity and understanding of congregational dynamics.

Further, these strengths are under the control of congregations. Congregations have little influence over location, worshiper demographics, and many congregational features.

Yet congregational leaders can focus on these important strengths and make changes to build up their abilities in these areas. The lesson here is that one strength, no matter how theologically central or significant, does not produce numerical growth or vitality.

Our findings are consistent with some current advice. Bill Easum declares, "The day of cloning is coming to an end."[3] He refers to the attempt by congregations to become just like highly successful churches such as Saddleback Church (Lake Forest, California) or Willow Creek Community Church (Chicago area). He advises leaders to "find God's model for your own environment" and "get to know your niche." Tim Keel, leader of Kansas City's Jacob's Well and one of the founders of the emergent church movement, echoes this advice by urging churches "to be 'environmentalists'—to take the temperature of their particular place and serve it accordingly."[4]

Thinking about Location as a Giant Turtle

The places where we live, work, and worship steal our hearts over time. Memories of people and events are "placed"—the significant events in our lives happen in particular places. Because we delight in the mystery and meaning of places, are we open to scientific explanations of how location affects our congregation?

A famous astronomer gave a public lecture several decades ago.[5] He did his best to plainly portray the vastness and beauty of our galaxy—interactions of sun, moon, and stars. When he finished his talk, an older woman approached him and said: "What you have said is rubbish! The world is really a flat plane supported on the back of a giant turtle." The scientist gave a surprisingly quick reply: "Well, what is the turtle standing on?" She snapped her answer: "You're very clever, young man, very clever. But it's turtles all the way down!"

A turtles-all-the-way-down view of the universe seems laughable. But all of us embrace soothing explanations that are not grounded in reality. Location explanations are like that. Many congregational leaders are certain that location is the big turtle upon which all congregational vitality rests. We've tried to oust the location turtle underlying most thinking about how place works for congregations. Our results show the relative unimportance of location compared to features internal to the congregation in predicting either congregational vitality or growth. But we're prepared to hear that it's turtles all the way down.

Base good decisions on observed reality.

Conclusion

God was in this place and I knew it not.

JACOB (BASED ON GEN. 28:16)

Congregational vitality is not captive to location. Describing the precise role that location plays in effective ministry is anything but simple. As we've demonstrated, some community factors turn out to be irrelevant for congregational strength. But some community features prove to be quite powerful and important for vital ministry.

Time and again, our results show that the single most important dynamic predicting vitality is the congregation's denomination or faith family. The congregation's faith-group affiliation points to the importance of theology, values, and the activities of worshipers that stem from those beliefs. Local theology (how the congregation applies the historical gospel to its current circumstances) directs the degree to which congregations engage with their communities or isolate themselves from certain age or cultural groups.

The second most important dynamic predicting strength is whether the percentage of 18- to 44-year-olds in the congregation mirrors the community's percentage of people in this age group. Congregations that reach out to this age group make their ministry relevant to today's young adults—the most underrepresented demographic group in religious life. This generation needs the congregation for spiritual formation and support during the critical first decades of adulthood. The congregation needs this generation's leadership now and for the future.

Each of the ten congregational strengths tends to be found in a unique set of locations and in congregations with specific internal features. In appendix 8 we summarize our findings for each congregational strength. We identify where each strength was typical or characteristic—by congregational location, the match between worshiper and community residents 18 to 44 years of age, the size of the congregation, the congregation's faith family, and the age profile of current worshipers. The summary in appendix 8 also shows the locations and types of congregations where each strength is less likely to be found. These strengths are challenges for local congregations in those locales. Such congregations may require greater attention to strategic planning and action to become stronger in these areas.

Are All Swans White?

Books, articles, and consultants regularly tell us the stories of successful congregations. While these congregational anecdotes may be inspiring, rarely can the strategies employed by these congregations be applied everywhere. Why is this true? The eighteenth-century philosopher David Hume called this reasoning error the black swan problem. He asked how many white swans must be observed before one can infer that all swans are white. We can't answer that question. Until people discovered black swans in Australia, all swans were believed to be white because all *observed* swans had been white. People took those observed facts and incorrectly generalized to all other swans.

The black swan problem arises when we derive general rules from observed facts. Until a fact emerges that contradicts the general rule—and we don't know when that anomaly might occur—we make incorrect assumptions. In any given sample of congregations (the ones we've had the opportunity to observe), random factors figure in. How can we know for sure what explains a congregation's success? Is it random fortune or the congregation's intentional strategies? Until we find a congregation that disproves the rule, we cannot know for sure if we have derived from our observations an accurate general rule.

In spite of this problem, as the number of observations (in our case, of congregations) increases, the likelihood also increases of identifying some underlying causal features. Further, we've observed a wide variety of congregational types and locations that enable us to discover some common threads. These causes will probably vary within categories of congregations, such as rural Protestant congregations in the Midwest or Catholic parishes in the South.

Every congregation is a niche congregation to a degree—attracting worshipers from a specific demographic slice, faith tradition, and location. For example, a Catholic parish in the Northeast may reach out to recent immigrants as well as cradle Catholics, but rarely draws Protestants into its ministry. A rural Lutheran congregation may offer a distinctly different ministry—relating to Protestant worshipers over an entire county perhaps. A downtown church may identify a ministry with a special population—persons with disabilities, for example—and draw worshipers from all over the city. A single congregation never serves all of God's people.

Congregations should refrain from applying general principles that may not fit their location. The best investment for those seeking to strengthen a congregation is (a) identifying the congregation's unique strengths, and (b) prayerfully discerning what God is calling the congregation to be and do *in this place*.

This book challenges congregations to think in new ways about their location—identifying as unique strengths elements of their location. New information is only one piece of that process. Unfortunately, untested assumptions and perceptions may crowd out valuable essentials because congregations have already formed a script—a way of viewing their location.

Every Congregation Has a Script about Its Location[1]

Congregations have scripts (ways of viewing and explaining reality) about many topics. What worshipers say to each other and to outsiders about their congregation's location is just one of those scripts. Sometimes the script is explicit, and a majority of worshipers make the same location assertions. However, the script often remains implicit. In these instances, the majority of worshipers *act* on similar beliefs about their location, even though those beliefs are never stated.

The congregation's location script may contain positive statements, perceptions, and feelings:

- "We have an ideal location near the highway."

- "We have a central location and plenty of parking."

- "Our property value is incredible. We couldn't buy this place now with today's prices."

The congregation's location script may contain negative statements, perceptions, and feelings:

- "We have an undesirable location, near . . ."

- "We have no room to expand. We need more places to park."

- "We are losing population in the area. We can't grow here."

- "The neighborhood has really changed. Most of our members have moved away."

Why do congregations have a location script? Scripts are necessary for the congregation's identity. They help congregations answer important questions: Who are we? What is our mission? The script identifies the congregation's goals, helps cement a sense of purpose, and supplies a feeling of security. Yet the congregation's location script can either fit or be at odds with the congregation's present core values.

A Congregation's Script Arises from Its History, Experiences, Tradition, and Untested Assumptions

The year and reason for the congregation's founding make up one part of the script. Typically, the location seemed perfect at the time the congregation was organized:

- "We were the first church organized in the county."

- "We're a new church start that began in the city's rapidly growing fringe."

- "Our congregation was born when two churches merged several years ago."

The congregation has experiences—profound and mundane—that contribute to the script:

- "Our church was destroyed by a fire. We had to decide whether to rebuild at the same place, close, or build someplace else."

- "Nothing much changes around here. We just remain faithful."

- "We were forced to relocate because the state wanted to build a highway through our parking lot."

- "This church is where famous people get married or have their funerals."

- "St. Paul's Chapel across from the World Trade Center towers became a place of prayer and refuge for rescue workers after the tragic events of September 11."

Traditions specific to a denomination or faith group contribute another ingredient for the script. Catholic parishes think differently about their location than do Seventh-day Adventist churches, for example. Catholic parishes focus on a location with clear geographic boundaries (the bounds of the parish), while conservative Protestant churches are free to define their ministry boundaries as broadly or as narrowly as they wish.

In the previous chapters, we've reviewed several untested assumptions or myths that congregations weave into their location script. For example, worshipers may assume that their congregation cannot attract new members because local population growth has plateaued. Congregational leaders may fail to acknowledge the significance of worship services that appeal to people younger than 45 years of age. Instead, they may blame irrelevant community characteristics for their current situation. In the end, the congregation's location script is a large chunk of its identity. The location script summarizes what we are about *in this place*. Who creates the script? Did the congregation write it? Yes, and they can change it.

Larger Cultural Scripts Influence a Congregation's Script

Biblical scholar Walter Brueggemann asserts that a dominant American script shapes individuals and faith communities.[2] He says this big script is based on therapeutic, technological, and consumerist assumptions. The therapeutic assumption common in America holds that any pain, discomfort, or inconvenience can be fixed through a product, treatment, or process. Congregations buy into this myth when they assume their problems can be fixed by a new location. This "grass-is-always-greener" view idealizes other locations: "Surely, congregations in other locations don't have our problems." Congregations that believe a "perfect" location exists somewhere, just not here, subscribe to this view. Dreaming about a new location with no trade-offs is a pleasant delusion.

The technological assumption underlying the American script reflects the belief that any issue or difficulty can be addressed through something we can create, like new technology. Congregations buy into this myth when they assume their problems will be over when they get the latest computer software, a congregational Web site, or an expensive projection system to make worship more meaningful or up-to-date. The technological assumption leads to believing that using technology will override the disadvantages of a congregation's present location.

The consumerist assumption behind our dominant script emerges in the American drive to buy, use, and then throw away virtually everything. Congregations buy into this myth when they treat their location as any other consumer product. If this location no longer works for us, then we can sell it and buy a new site. Viewing the congregation's location as a commodity means we use it without regard for how our use might impact others.

A Congregation's Location Script May Hinder More Than It Helps

What are the symptoms that a congregation's script is failing? Its location script is out of touch with current reality and has lost its relevance. The congregation no longer sees its location as God-given, a promise, an aspect of mission, or a strength. Congregations at this stage of script failure find their thinking limits their perceptions. They read their

DO WE BELIEVE IN MIRACLES OR MAGIC?

Most of us *say* we believe in miracles, but our *actions* show we believe in magic.[3] When facing a challenging, seemingly impossible situation, what is the difference between putting our faith in magic rather than miracles?

We put our faith in *magic* when . . .

- We aren't willing to change.
- We take no risks.
- We pray for God to fix it for us.
- We take no action and wait for something to happen.
- We are disappointed when nothing changes.

We place our faith in *miracles* when . . .

- We are realistic about the facts.
- We are willing to take risks and make sacrifices.
- We open our hearts, seeking to know the change to which God is calling us.
- We discover that God is with us in the risk.

"symptoms" as reality. To grow stronger requires that the congregation disengage from and relinquish their failed location script. Why would a congregation hold onto a script that blocks growth and promotes self-fulfilling results? Because the current script, despite its warts, grants some benefits. To embrace a new script means leaving behind a comfortable old script and accepting the emotional losses that accompany change.

Does this mean every congregation should remain in its current location? Probably not. A new, alternative script may involve relocating to another site that better fits the current mission, values, and strengths of the congregation. Sometimes congregations feel called to another location where their traditions and ministry build on the promise of an alternative site. Others see that continued decline would result if they remain in their current location. Congregations struggle with such a dramatic decision. Yet, in some cases, relocation can be the wisest and most faithful response to what God is calling them to be and do as a congregation.

Congregational Leaders Must Encourage the Revision of Location Scripts

Courageous leaders appeal to the existing script as a footbridge to the future. They find ways to celebrate the past but truthfully pinpoint how the existing script is not working. These leaders show how current views about location are inconsistent with the congregation's theology, values, tradition, and present reality. They find ways to challenge the existing script and its legitimacy. They convince others that the congregation will not move forward if it relies on the old script. A congregation that acknowledges the neighborhood has changed, for example, can begin to create a new script that seeks to use existing congregational strengths to accommodate that change.

Leaders Must Articulate an Alternative Script That Leads to Seeing the Promise of Place

All places belong to God. Only for a time are places entrusted to us. In the most fundamental sense, congregations didn't purchase their land, nor do they own it—their location is their birthright. As Brueggemann makes clear, the alternative understanding runs counter to the dominant cultural script:

> The claim of that alternative script is that there is at work among us a Truth that makes us safe, . . . free, and . . . joyous in a way that the comfort and ease of the consumer economy cannot even imagine.[4]

The Alternative Location Script Is Multidimensional, but Never Perfectly Complete

A congregation's refined location script should be a general description that:

- allows God to fill in the details
- allows for change and an openness to God's continuing work in the world
- recognizes the tension between our understanding that God is everywhere and yet is here *in this place* for a specific purpose
- acknowledges our ambivalence about embracing an alternative script
- doesn't create a crisis but names the crisis we're already in
- calls for continuing critical reflection about how our location shapes our congregation's ministry
- claims our location as an inherited birthright

One of the Chosen Venues for the Work of God's Spirit Is between the Old and New Scripts

God's Spirit meets us in the gap between our past script and our promising future. This is the time when leaders and members are most open to new possibilities. Illusions as well as any sense of entitlement fall away. Finally, we can make room for a new vision about our location and embrace its covenantal requirements. Jeremiah, who made a down payment on behalf of God, reminds us of how God redeems people and places when we are determined to thrive in the community where God planted us. When we are willing to accept the irrational and seemingly unbearable assignment—"buy a piece of land in the heart of Jerusalem" or wherever God calls us to be—God transforms us, transforms our congregation, transforms our community, and transforms the world.

THE INTERNATIONAL CONGREGATIONAL LIFE SURVEY

The International Congregational Life Survey (ICLS) was initiated in 1999 as a collaborative effort of four countries. The ICLS extends the National Church Life Survey (NCLS) used earlier in Australia and aims to provide mission resources for congregations and parishes based on results from a survey of church attenders in four nations. The ICLS project was conducted in April and May 2001, with more than twelve thousand congregations and 1.2 million worshipers participating. Each congregation invited all worshipers to complete a survey. The congregations also completed a congregational profile form, and the key leader in each congregation answered questions as well. Survey results are being used to provide individualized reports to each participating congregation and to produce books, research reports, and other resources about religious life in the twenty-first century.

The ICLS was conducted by the following agencies and people:

Australia: National Church Life Survey (NCLS; http://www.ncls.org.au/), sponsored by ANGLICARE NSW of the Anglican Church in Australia, the New South Wales Board of Mission of the Uniting Church in Australia, and the Australian Catholic Bishops Conference: Dean Drayton (convener of the ICLS steering committee), John Bellamy,

Keith Castle, Howard Dillon,* Robert Dixon, Peter Kaldor (founding director of NCLS), Ruth Powell, Tina Rendell,* and Sam Sterland.

England: Churches Information for Mission (CIM): Phillip Escott, Alison Gelder,* Roger Whitehead.*

New Zealand: Church Life Survey–New Zealand (CLS-NZ) is a subcommittee of the Christian Research Association of New Zealand: Norman Brookes.*

United States: U.S. Congregations supported by Lilly Endowment, Inc., the Louisville Institute, and the Research Services office of the Presbyterian Church (U.S.A.): Deborah Bruce, Cynthia Woolever,* Keith Wulff,* Ida Smith-Williams.

*ICLS Steering Committee

U.S. Congregational Life Survey Methodology

Over three hundred thousand worshipers in more than two thousand congregations across America participated in the U.S. Congregational Life Survey—making it the largest survey of worshipers in America ever conducted. Three types of surveys were completed in each participating congregation: (a) an attendee survey completed by all worshipers age 15 and older who attended worship services during the weekend of April 29, 2001; (b) a congregational profile describing the congregation's facilities, staff, programs, and worship services, completed by one person in the congregation; and (c) a leader survey completed by the pastor, priest, minister, rabbi, or other leader. Together the information collected provides a unique three-dimensional look at religious life in America.

The National Opinion Research Center (NORC) at the University of Chicago identified a random sample of U.S. congregations attended by individuals who participated in the General Social Survey (GSS) in the year 2000. All GSS participants who reported that they attended worship at least once in the prior year were asked to name the place where they worshiped. Since the GSS involves a national random sample of individuals, congregations identified by GSS participants comprise a national random sample of congregations. NORC researchers verified that each nominated congregation was an actual congregation and then invited each congregation to participate in the project. Of 1,214 nominated and verified congregations, 807 agreed to participate (66%), and 434 returned completed surveys from their worshipers (36%). (Congregations that chose not to participate gave a wide variety of reasons.) Worshipers in these congregations, representing all fifty states, completed 122,043 attendee surveys, which are the primary source of the findings reported here. The size of this scientific statistical sample far exceeds the size of most national surveys. Studies designed to provide a representative profile of adults living in the United States typically include about a thousand people.

Denominations were also invited and encouraged to draw a random sample of their congregations. Denominational samples were large enough so that the results are representative of worshipers and congregations in each denomination. This allows denominations to compare their "typical" congregation and worshiper to congregations and worshipers in other denominations. Denominations participating in this oversampling procedure were: Church of the Nazarene, Evangelical Lutheran Church in America (ELCA), Presbyterian Church (U.S.A.), Roman Catholic Church, Seventh-day Adventist Church, Southern Baptist Convention, United Methodist Church (UMC), and United Church of Christ (UCC). In subsequent years, three other groups participated: a random sample of fast-growing churches in the ELCA, a random sample of fast-growing churches in the Presbyterian Church (U.S.A.), and a random sample of congregations in the Episcopal Church. In addition, the Interdenominational Theological Center (ITC) used the U.S. Congregational Life Survey with samples of predominantly black Protestant churches, Catholic parishes, and mosques. Finally, many individual congregations and small groups of congregations have taken the survey. (See appendix 9 for details about taking the survey.) Results from these other samples are not included here.

Additional information about the methods used in this study is available on our Web site: http://www.USCongregations.org.

QUESTIONS AND ANSWERS ABOUT THE U.S. CONGREGATIONAL LIFE SURVEY

What Level of Analysis Was Used?

Information in *A Field Guide to U.S. Congregations*[1] was based on surveys completed by worshipers (individual-level analyses). In *Beyond the Ordinary*[2] and in this book, we've aggregated the responses of individual worshipers to the congregational level (congregational-level analyses). We combined responses from all worshipers in each congregation to see what they say as a group about their congregation. We also weighted the congregational-level data to account for size and nonresponse biases. Because congregations were nominated for participation in this study by a random sample of adults, larger congregations (with so many more worshipers) were more likely to have been nominated. The weights we used counterbalanced this bias. Similarly, certain denominations and faith groups were under-represented in the sample, and the weights also corrected for this bias.

All three books include some results from information that was provided on the congregational profile—the survey completed by one person in each congregation describing the congregation's programs, services, facilities, staff, and finances.

Where Did the Information about the Religious Composition of Regions and Communities Come From?

This information comes from the Glenmary Research Center's *Religious Congregations and Membership in the United States 2000*. Beginning in 1952 and approximately every ten years since, church and church membership data have been compiled to approximate a census of American religion. For the 2000 volume, all religious groups listed in the 1999 *Yearbook of American and Canadian Churches* were invited to report the number of their congregations, the number of individuals with full membership status, and the group's "total adherents" (defined as "all members, including full members, their children, and the estimated number of other participants who are not considered members") in each county of the country. Because religious groups define membership in a variety of ways, figures for total adherents are more comparable across denominations and religious groups. The statistics are usefully reported at multiple geographic levels—counties, states, census regions, and nationally. While not all religious groups supplied data, the RCMS represents about 89% of all adherents. (This information is available online at: http://www.thearda.com.)

Where Can I Learn More about the Red-State/Blue-State and Red-County/Blue-County Divide?

Wikipedia, an online encyclopedia, provides a history of the red and blue state or county divide. (This information is available online at: http://en.wikipedia.org/wiki/red_states).

Where Did the Community Information Come From?

This information comes from the 2000 U.S. Census. First, the physical location of each participating congregation was identified (through geo-coding). Then the census tracts within a three-mile radius of the congregation's location were identified to capture census information about the people and housing in those tracts. (Census information is available online at: http://factfinder.census.gov.)

How Were the Ten Strengths Identified?

The ten strengths in *Beyond the Ordinary* and this book tap the essential strengths of congregations. We believe that all congregations possess strengths, and this multifaceted approach allows congregations to find the areas in which they excel. Also, we're indebted to many congregational and denominational leaders, church consultants, and religious researchers who helped us inventory the characteristics of healthy and vital congregations. For more information about the strengths, see *Beyond the Ordinary* (particularly appendix 2).

Can I Compare the Scores across Strengths?

No. Because the questions that make up each index use widely different scales, they cannot be compared. That is, just because the average score on the Growing Spiritually Index is higher than the average score on the Meaningful Worship Index does *not* mean that congregations in general are doing better in the area of spirituality than in the area of worship. It *is* appropriate to compare the scores of congregations in different locations on one index—for example, comparing congregations in the West to those in the Northeast on the Growing Spiritually Index.

How Were the Denominational Families Established?

The denominational families used in this book represent a common typology of congregations used by religion researchers. Congregations within each family are fairly similar to one another in terms of theology and belief, and less similar to congregations in other faith groups. Appendix 5 shows the specific denominations participating in the U.S. Congregational Life Survey that fall in each category.

How Was Congregational Growth Measured?

Each participating congregation completed a congregational profile, which asked for the average annual worship attendance for the past five years (1996 to 2001). Because the survey was given in April 2001, worship attendance figures for that year were incomplete, and some congregations did not report that figure. Growth was measured as an average of two measures of the annual percentage of growth or decline in worship attendance: (a) between 1996 and 2000 (attendance in 2000 minus attendance in 1996, the difference divided by attendance in 1996) and (b) between 1996 and 2001. Thus, positive numbers indicate a congregation has more worshipers in 2000 or 2001 than in 1996, and negative numbers indicate fewer worshipers. Some congregations did not report attendance figures for 1996 and/or for 2000. In such cases, growth was calculated based on the earliest and latest reported attendance figures.

Can My Congregation Take the Survey?

Yes, you can! If you would like to see how your congregation compares with the U.S. results, or get help identifying your congregation's strengths, see appendix 9 for information about taking the survey.

STRENGTHS BY FAITH GROUP AND SURVEY QUESTIONS COMPRISING THE STRENGTH MEASURES

Strength	Total n=434		Catholic n=100		Mainline Protestant n=180		Conservative Protestant n=129	
	Mean	SD	Mean	SD	Mean	SD	Mean	SD
Growing Spiritually (Cronbach's alpha = .77)	**47%**	**10.9**	**38%**	**4.9**	**41%**	**7.6**	**55%**	**8.6**
Report much growth in faith through participation in activities of the congregation	43%	18.7	32%	13.4	35%	11.7	53%	19.8
Spend time at least a few times a week in private devotions	72%	15.7	61%	8.1	64%	14.3	82%	11.8
Feel that their spiritual needs are being met in the congregation	84%	10.0	83%	6.0	81%	12.7	87%	6.6
Report Bible study and prayer groups are one of three most valued aspects of the congregation	21%	16.0	9%	7.3	12%	9.3	31%	15.8
Report prayer ministry of the congregation is one of three most valued aspects of the congregation	16%	13.6	5%	3.7	12%	8.1	23%	15.7

Strength	Total n=434		Catholic n=100		Mainline Protestant n=180		Conservative Protestant n=129	
	Mean	SD	Mean	SD	Mean	SD	Mean	SD
Meaningful Worship (Cronbach's alpha = .86)	**62%**	**11.4**	**58%**	**9.6**	**56%**	**9.5**	**69%**	**9.6**
Always or usually experience God's presence during services	78%	18.1	83%	8.8	68%	21.0	85%	11.0
Always or usually experience inspiration during services	78%	14.9	70%	15.3	70%	13.5	86%	11.1
Rarely experience boredom during services	69%	16.6	59%	12.7	66%	11.6	75%	18.4
Always or usually experience awe during services	25%	12.8	34%	16.2	21%	9.8	27%	13.2
Always or usually experience joy during services	79%	14.9	72%	11.1	72%	16.0	87%	10.4
Rarely experience frustration during services	73%	14.8	67%	12.0	69%	12.8	78%	15.9
Report worship helps them with everyday life	56%	19.9	43%	12.4	44%	14.5	69%	17.6
Report sermons or homilies are one of the three most valued aspects of the congregation	39%	14.8	32%	12.0	37%	12.2	44%	15.6
Participating in the Congregation (Cronbach's alpha = .82)	**60%**	**13.4**	**44%**	**9.9**	**55%**	**9.5**	**69%**	**10.1**
Attend worship services usually every week or more often	81%	14.4	80%	8.7	73%	13.6	89%	9.5
Are involved in one or more small groups (e.g., Sunday school, prayer or Bible study, discussion groups, fellowships)	67%	19.6	42%	14.9	60%	15.9	78%	15.4
Hold one or more leadership roles in the congregation (e.g., board member, teacher, leading worship)	57%	13.8	42%	15.6	56%	11.1	60%	12.6
Often participate in decision making in the congregation	33%	16.8	14%	10.4	30%	9.8	40%	18.9
Give 5% or more of net income to the congregation	63%	21.5	44%	15.1	53%	19.6	77%	13.3
Sense of Belonging (Cronbach's alpha = .74)	**37%**	**11.4**	**30%**	**10.3**	**31%**	**6.3**	**43%**	**11.9**
Have a strong and growing sense of belonging to the congregation	58%	17.0	48%	13.5	51%	12.5	66%	17.4
Report most of their closest friends attend the same congregation	19%	11.8	15%	7.7	12%	6.0	25%	13.3
Participate in congregational activities more now, than two years ago	33%	12.8	27%	14.8	28%	8.7	37%	13.9

Strength	Total n=434		Catholic n=100		Mainline Protestant n=180		Conservative Protestant n=129	
	Mean	SD	Mean	SD	Mean	SD	Mean	SD
Caring for Children and Youth (Cronbach's alpha = .65)	**50%**	**12.5**	**46%**	**7.3**	**49%**	**12.3**	**53%**	**13.1**
Are satisfied with offerings for children and youth	58%	20.7	54%	14.8	56%	20.7	61%	21.7
Report ministry for children or youth is one of three most valued aspects of the congregation	16%	11.8	9%	4.7	16%	9.8	18%	14.3
Report that children and youth living at home worship in the same congregation	77%	17.8	74%	13.5	76%	17.0	81%	18.0
Focusing on the Community (Cronbach's alpha = .81)	**33%**	**8.9**	**33%**	**7.2**	**38%**	**8.7**	**28%**	**6.9**
Are involved in social service or advocacy groups through the congregation	26%	14.1	20%	9.3	30%	11.0	24%	16.2
Are involved in social service or advocacy groups outside the congregation	28%	13.8	28%	8.7	36%	10.5	20%	13.0
Contributed money to a charitable group other than the congregation	66%	13.9	65%	17.7	73%	11.6	60%	12.7
Report the congregation's wider community care and advocacy are one of the three most valued aspects of the congregation	11%	10.9	14%	10.1	16%	13.2	6%	6.2
Report the congregation's openness to social diversity is one of the three most valued aspects of the congregation	8%	13.3	10%	8.7	14%	18.7	3%	5.0
Worked with others to try to solve a community problem in the past year	21%	10.0	23%	9.1	23%	10.9	18%	8.9
Voted in 2000 presidential election	71%	15.9	70%	14.6	78%	11.4	66%	17.2
Sharing Faith (Cronbach's alpha = .90)	**32%**	**14.6**	**20%**	**8.2**	**23%**	**8.2**	**43%**	**12.2**
Are involved in evangelism activities of the congregation	23%	13.6	11%	8.6	17%	9.0	31%	13.1
Feel at ease talking about their faith and seek opportunities to do so	24%	16.3	17%	9.1	12%	6.9	36%	15.4
Have invited a friend or relative to worship in past year	60%	20.9	40%	12.8	49%	14.9	75%	16.5
Report ministry to the unchurched is one of the three most valued aspects of the congregation	22%	15.9	12%	7.4	13%	10.1	32%	16.2

Strength	Total n=434		Catholic n=100		Mainline Protestant n=180		Conservative Protestant n=129	
	Mean	SD	Mean	SD	Mean	SD	Mean	SD
Welcoming New People: Percentage of worshipers who began attending in the past five years	**33%**	**17.4**	**27%**	**12.3**	**29%**	**13.2**	**39%**	**20.1**
Empowering Leadership (Cronbach's alpha = .84)	**49%**	**15.9**	**39%**	**13.4**	**44%**	**14.4**	**57%**	**14.9**
Feel the congregation's leaders encourage them to use their gifts	41%	16.4	30%	14.8	34%	11.3	50%	15.2
Feel the leader takes into account the ideas of others	54%	17.8	45%	15.6	52%	16.6	58%	18.9
Describe the leadership style of the pastor or priest as one that inspires others	50%	18.6	39%	15.1	47%	18.2	56%	18.1
Believe there is a good match between the pastor or priest and the congregation	53%	24.1	42%	17.8	42%	23.5	63%	22.4
Looking to the Future (Cronbach's alpha = .82)	**41%**	**13.2**	**34%**	**6.2**	**35%**	**12.1**	**47%**	**12.7**
Feel the congregation has a clear vision and goals that they are strongly committed to	42%	18.9	26%	12.5	32%	13.2	55%	16.3
Have a sense of excitement about the congregation's future	33%	17.4	34%	4.7	23%	14.4	40%	18.5
Believe the congregation is already moving in new directions	32%	18.7	27%	11.0	31%	15.4	34%	22.0
Believe the congregation is always ready to try new things	56%	18.8	50%	3.9	54%	16.3	59%	22.6

Note: Cronbach's alpha is a measure of reliability of the strength index, that is, how well the survey questions used together measure the strength.

SD = standard deviation, the variability of scores. A higher standard deviation indicates more variability.

Mean is the average across all scores.

DENOMINATIONAL FAMILIES

The denominational families used in this book represent a common typology of congregations used by religion researchers. The specific denominations participating in the U.S. Congregational Life Survey that fall in each category are shown below. Because the "other" category is so broad (including Jewish synagogues, Buddhist temples, and other non-Christian faiths) and because the number of historically black churches is so small, we do not report means for these groups separately in the book. All congregations were included in analyses used to develop the strength indices and are included in the overall scores we report, but these two groups were excluded from the analyses by faith group. The unweighted numbers of congregations included in the analyses for this book in each denominational family are 100 Catholic parishes, 180 mainline Protestant churches, 129 conservative Protestant churches, 9 historically black churches, and 12 congregations of other types.

Catholic Churches

Roman Catholic

Mainline Protestant Churches

American Baptist Churches USA
Baptist Bible Fellowship, International
Christian Church (Disciples of Christ)
Christian Reformed Church in North
America
Episcopal Church
Episcopal/Anglican (unspecified)
Evangelical Lutheran Church in
America

Greek Orthodox
Lutheran (unspecified)
Presbyterian (unspecified)
Presbyterian Church (U.S.A.)
Unitarian Universalist Association
United Church of Christ
United Methodist Church
Unity of the Brethren (Moravian)

Conservative Protestant Churches

Assemblies of God
Baptist (unspecified)
Christian and Missionary Alliances
Christian Churches and Churches of
Christ
Christian Churches of North America
Church of God
Church of God (Anderson, Indiana)
Church of God (Cleveland, Tennessee)
Church of the Nazarene
Churches of Christ
Conservative Baptist Association of
America

Conservative Congregational Christian
Conference
Foursquare Gospel
Free Methodist Church of North
America
Free Will Baptist
General Association of Regular Baptist
Church
Lutheran Church, Missouri Synod
Mennonite (unspecified)
Mennonite Church
Missionary
Nondenominational

Nondenominational Evangelical
Nondenominational Pentecostal
Pentecostal (unspecified)
Presbyterian Church in America
Seventh-day Adventist
Southern Baptist Convention

United Baptist
United Pentecostal Church,
    International
Unity School of Christianity
Wesleyan Church

Historically Black Churches

African Methodist Episcopal Zion
    Church

Church of God in Christ
National Baptist Convention, USA

Other Congregations

Buddhist Communities
Church of Jesus Christ of Latter-day
    Saints
Conservative Judaism
Judaism (unspecified)

Nondenominational, Non-Christian
Reform Judaism
Reorganized Church of Jesus Christ of
    Latter-day Saints

COMMUNITY VARIABLES FROM THE U.S. CENSUS

All community variables come from the 2000 U.S. Census and describe the people and housing in the census tracts within a three-mile radius of each participating congregation's location.

Population: The number of people living in the local community.

Population change: The change in population in the area between 1990 and 2000, as a percentage of 1990 population.

Urban population: The percentage of the population living in urban areas. Urban areas generally consist of a large central place (with population density of 1,000 people per square mile) and adjacent densely settled areas (with population density of 500 people per square mile) that together have a total population of at least 2,500 for urban clusters, or at least 50,000 for urbanized areas.

Age: The age of each person as of April 1, 2000. Used to group the population into the following age ranges (some of which were combined for particular analyses):

Under 18: The percentage of people under age 18.

18–29: The percentage of people age 18 to 29.

30–44: The percentage of people age 30 to 44.

45–64: The percentage of people age 45 to 64.

65+: The percentage of people age 65 and older.

Foreign-born: The percentage of people in the community who were not U.S. citizens at birth. This includes immigrants (legal permanent residents and naturalized citizens), temporary migrants (e.g., students), humanitarian migrants (e.g., refugees), and unauthorized migrants (e.g., people illegally residing in the United States).

Race/ethnicity: Self-identified race (white, black or African American, American Indian or Alaska Native, Asian, Native Hawaiian or Other Pacific Islander, or some other race) and ethnicity (Hispanic or non-Hispanic).

Minority: Percentage of the population who are other than non-Hispanic white.

Educational attainment: The highest degree or level of education completed by people in the local community. Reported only for those 25 years of age and older.

No high school: The percentage of the population who did not earn a high school degree or an equivalency (e.g., GED).

High school: The percentage of the population who completed high school or an equivalency (e.g., GED).

Post-secondary: The percentage of the population who are high school graduates with some years of college or an associate degree.

College degree: The percentage of the population who completed a bachelor's, master's, doctoral, or professional degree.

Employment status: Reported only for those 16 years of age and older.

Employed: The percentage of the population who are working as paid employees; in own business or a profession; or on a family farm or in a family business.

Unemployed: The percentage of the population who are able to work but not at work, looking for work, or on temporary layoff from a job.

Not in labor force: The percentage of the population who are not in the work force—retired, students, taking care of home or family, institutionalized, and so on.

Occupation: Reported only for those 16 years of age and older.

Working professionals: The percentage of the civilian labor force age 16 and over employed in professional or managerial occupations.

Working in service industry: The percentage of the civilian labor force age 16 and over employed in service, sales, and office occupations.

Working in farming/construction/production industries: The percentage of the civilian labor force age 16 and over employed in farming, production, construction, and similar occupations.

Household type: The household composition of people who occupy a housing unit. Excludes those in group housing (nursing homes, correctional institutions, college dorms, military housing).

Married-couple family with children: The percentage of households with a married couple living with one or more of their children under age 18 at home.

Married-couple family without children: The percentage of households with a married couple.

Female-headed household: The percentage of households with a female head (no husband present) and one or more of her children under age 18 living at home.

Income: Total income from wages or salary, self-employment, interest, dividends, social security and retirement pensions, public assistance, and all other income in the previous year (1999).

Average household income: Computed by aggregating household income for householders age 15 and over (whether related or not) and dividing by the number of households.

Poverty: The percentage of people in households living in poverty. The measure of poverty is based on total family income relative to poverty threshold for family size and composition. (Excludes those in group housing.)

Mobility: The percentage of the population age 5 and older not living in the same house as in 1995.

Housing: Information about living quarters (e.g., house, apartment, mobile home, boat, etc.).

Owner-occupied housing: The percentage of housing units that are owner-occupied (as opposed to those that are rental units), whether the unit is fully owned or owned with a mortgage.

New housing: The percentage of housing units built after 1995.

WHERE ARE THE COMMUNITY TYPES FOUND?

	Rural	Growing Suburban	Small Cities and Stable Suburban	Economically Distressed Urban	High-Mobility Urban
Northeast	11%	19%	25%	7%	12%
Midwest	**41%**	15%	26%	14%	24%
South	**43%**	**38%**	24%	**59%**	**38%**
West	5%	**28%**	26%	19%	26%
Total	100%	100%	101%	99%	100%
Bible Belt	**53%**	36%	22%	**61%**	39%
Rest of U.S.	47%	**64%**	**78%**	39%	**61%**
Total	100%	100%	100%	100%	100%
Blue State	28%	**59%**	43%	25%	32%
Red State	**72%**	41%	**57%**	**75%**	**68%**
Total	100%	100%	100%	100%	100%

Note: Read this table column by column. Each column shows where congregations in particular community types tend to be found. Bold numbers indicate the community type is more common in that region. For example, the bold numbers in the first column indicate that congregations in Rural communities tend to be found in the Midwest (41%) and South (43%), in the Bible Belt (53%), and in Red States (72%).

LOCATION AND STRENGTH: SUMMARY OF WHICH CONGREGATIONS TEND TO HAVE STRENGTHS

Strength	This strength is characteristic of congregations that are:	This strength is a challenge for congregations that are:
Growing Spiritually	Midwest, South	Northeast, West
	Red state	Blue state
	Red county	Blue county
	Bible Belt	Outside Bible Belt
	Churched counties	Less churched counties
	Rural comunities	High-Mobility Urban communities
	Match on 18–44	
	Small	Large
	Conservative Protestant	Catholic, mainline Protestant
Meaningful Worship	Midwest, South	Northeast, West
	Red state	Blue state

Strength	This strength is characteristic of congregations that are:	This strength is a challenge for congregations that are:
Meaningful Worship (*continued*)	Red county	Blue county
	Bible Belt	Outside Bible Belt
	Churched counties	Less churched counties
	Rural communities	High-Mobility Urban communities
	Economically Distressed Urban communities	
	Match on 18–44	
	Conservative Protestant	Catholic, mainline Protestant
Participating in the Congregation	Midwest, South	Northeast, West
	Red state	Blue state
	Red county	Blue county
	Bible Belt	Outside Bible Belt
	Churched counties	Less churched counties
	Rural communities	High-Mobility Urban communities
	Small	Large
	Conservative Protestant	Catholic, mainline Protestant
Sense of Belonging	Midwest	Northeast, West
	Red state	Blue state
	Red county	Blue county
	Bible Belt	Outside Bible Belt
	Rural communities	High-Mobility Urban communities
	Match on 18–44	
	Small	Large
	Conservative Protestant	Catholic, mainline Protestant
	Younger worshipers	Older worshipers

Strength	This strength is characteristic of congregations that are:	This strength is a challenge for congregations that are:
Caring for Children and Youth	Churched counties	Less churched counties
	Rural areas, Growing Suburban communities	Economically Distressed Urban communities
	Small Cities/Stable Suburban	High-Mobility Urban communities
	Match on 18–44	
	Mid-size	Small or large
	Conservative Protestant	Catholic, mainline Protestant
	Younger worshipers	Older worshipers
Focusing on the Community	Northeast	Midwest, South
	Blue state	Red state
	Blue county	Red county
	Outside Bible Belt	Bible Belt
	Less churched counties	Churched counties
	Growing Suburban communities	Rural communities
	Small Cities/Stable Suburban communities	Economically Distressed Urban communities
	High-Mobility Urban areas	
	Mismatch on 18–44	
	Mainline Protestant	Catholic, conservative Protestant
	Older worshipers	Younger worshipers
Sharing Faith	South	Northeast, West
	Red state	Blue state
	Red county	Blue county
	Bible Belt	Outside Bible Belt
	Rural areas	High-Mobility Urban communities
	Economically Distressed Urban communities	

Strength	This strength is characteristic of congregations that are:	This strength is a challenge for congregations that are:
Sharing Faith (*continued*)	Match on 18–44	
	Small	Large
	Conservative Protestant	Catholic, mainline Protestant
Welcoming New People	West	Northeast
	Blue county	Red county
	Less churched counties	
	Growing Suburban communities	Economically Distressed Urban communities
		High-Mobility Urban communities
	Match on 18–44	
	Conservative Protestant	Catholic, mainline Protestant
	Younger worshipers	Older worshipers
Empowering Leadership	Midwest, South	West
	Red state	Blue state
	Bible Belt	Outside Bible Belt
	Rural areas	High-Mobility Urban communities
	Economically Distressed Urban communities	Small Cities/Stable Suburban communities
	Match on 18–44	
	Small	Large
	Conservative Protestant	Catholic, mainline Protestant
Looking to the Future	South	Northeast, West
	Red state	Blue state
	Bible Belt	Outside Bible Belt
	Match on 18–44	
	Conservative Protestant	Catholic, mainline Protestant
	Younger worshipers	Older worshipers

The U.S. Congregational Life Survey: A Tool for Discovering Your Congregation's Strengths

Why Conduct a Survey of Your Congregation?

- to find out who your worshipers are and what they value

- to consider new missions or programs

- to renew or reevaluate your strategic plan

- to deal with change when your congregation is growing or declining

- to get ready to call a new pastor

- to help a new pastor learn more about the congregation

Who Will See Your Answers?

They are completely confidential; unless you choose to share your results with others, no one outside your congregation will see them. You'll send your surveys directly back to our research office. We'll use an identification number to help us keep track of your congregation's responses, but individual answers are all confidential—in fact, we ask worshipers not to put their names on the survey. We'll combine the responses of all of your worshipers and provide summary reports telling you what they said.

How Should We Give the Survey? We Can't Afford to Mail It to Every Member.

The survey is designed to be given in worship on a typical Sunday or other day of worship. Giving the survey in worship is an efficient way to take a snapshot of your congregation, including regular worshipers, those who come less often, and visitors. If your congregation has more than one weekly service, the survey should be given in each one.

Who Should Participate?

Every worshiper who is at least 15 years old should take part in the survey, including ushers, members of the choir, and others who help lead the service.

How Much Time Will This Require?

Most worshipers can complete the survey in fifteen minutes. Each question is in a quick response format so that worshipers do not have to write out their answers. We suggest setting aside about twenty minutes to allow time for explaining, distributing, and collecting the surveys.

How Can We Fit It in Our Worship Service?

Congregations have found a variety of ways to give the survey in worship. Many have found that it works well to set aside the last twenty minutes of each scheduled worship service to distribute the survey. Then, worshipers can leave when they have finished. Our experience shows that if you let worshipers take the surveys home with them, few will return them. To make sure your portrait is accurate, it's essential to give the survey during worship.

When Should We Conduct the Survey?

It's your decision when to conduct the survey. Select the week that is most convenient for your congregation. It's best to pick a week that is typical. Giving the survey on Mother's Day or on a holiday weekend, for example, won't give you an accurate portrait if more visitors than normal attend or if many of your frequent attendees are away.

What Will We Get When We Participate?

- Two customized, color reports. One has detailed profiles of your worshipers—their involvement in the congregation and community, their values, and their hopes for the future. The other gives a detailed profile of your congregation and its unique strengths, especially compared to others of similar size and faith group.

- Two videos providing step-by-step instructions for interpreting the reports. They are designed to facilitate group discussion and help leaders identify congregational strengths.

- Two leader's guides with many helpful ideas and tools for making the most of your congregation's reports.

- Two books summarizing the key national findings: *A Field Guide to U.S. Congregations: Who Is Going Where and Why* and *Beyond the Ordinary: Ten Strengths of U.S. Congregations* (both published by Westminster John Knox Press).

What Will This Cost?

The current fees are listed on our Web site at http://www.USCongregations.org, or you may call 1-888-728-7228, ext. 2040, to learn more. We'll send you all the surveys you need (forms are available in English, Spanish, and Korean), pens to complete them, and instructions for giving the survey in worship. You'll need to pay for shipping to return the completed surveys to us for processing.

What about Other Questions We Have? How Can We Sign Up?

To obtain general information, visit http://www.uscongregations.org, or if you're ready to get started, please call us toll-free at 1-888-728-7228, ext. 2040.

What Is U.S. Congregations?

U.S. Congregations is a religious research group, housed in the offices of the Presbyterian Church (U.S.A.) in Louisville, Kentucky, staffed by religion researchers and sociologists who are conducting the U.S. Congregational Life Survey.

NOTES

Introduction

1. David Roozen, "Old-line Protestantism: Pockets of Vitality within a Continuing Stream of Decline" (Hartford Institute for Religion Research working paper 1104.1, Hartford Seminary, http://hirr.hartsem.edu/bookshelf/roozen_article5.html, 2004). The observation was attributed to H. Paul Douglas.
2. James Webb Young, *A Technique for Producing Ideas* (New York: McGraw-Hill, 2003), 25.
3. For more detail about these strengths, see Cynthia Woolever and Deborah Bruce, *Beyond the Ordinary: Ten Strengths of U.S. Congregations* (Louisville, KY: Westminster John Knox Press, 2004). For more details about the international research, see appendix 1 and publications based on the National Church Life Survey such as Peter Kaldor, Keith Castle, and Robert Dixon, *Connections for Life: Core Qualities to Foster in Your Church* (Adelaide, Australia: Openbook Publishers, 2002).
4. Appendix 2 details the U.S. Congregational Life Survey methodology, and appendix 3 provides answers to some questions about the data analyses used in this book. The strength measurement, Welcoming New People, is based on a single question and reflects the percentage of worshipers who began attending the congregation in the past five years.
5. The Association of Statisticians of American Religious Bodies (ASARB) sponsors this report, a compilation of statistics for 149 religious bodies, providing information on the number of their congregations within each region, state, and county of the United States. Additional information is given in appendix 3 and online at http://www.thearda.com.

6. Sheldon S. Wolin, *The Presence of the Past: Essays on the State and the Constitution* (Baltimore: Johns Hopkins University Press, 1989), 138.

7. These paragraphs draw heavily from a sermon preached by Ann J. Deibert, pastor of Central Presbyterian Church, Louisville, KY, on September 30, 2001—a few weeks after the September 11 attacks on the World Trade Center, the Pentagon, and Flight 93.

Chapter One: Strength in States and Regions

1. All census data used in this book are from the 2000 U.S. Census—the census closest in time to April 2001, when the U.S. Congregational Life Survey was conducted.

2. The percentages in this paragraph are derived from the Glenmary Research Center's *Religious Congregations and Membership in the United States 2000*. Approximately every ten years, church and church membership data are compiled by the Association of Statisticians of American Religious Bodies to approximate a census of American religion. For 2000, all religious groups listed in the 1999 *Yearbook of American and Canadian Churches* were invited to report the number of their congregations, the number of individuals with full membership status, and the group's "total adherents" (defined as "all members, including full members, their children, and the estimated number of other participants who are not considered members"). Because religious groups define membership in a variety of ways, total adherents figures are more comparable across groups. The statistics are available for counties, states, census regions, and nationally. The RCMS represents about 89% of all adherents because many historically black denominations and some smaller religious groups did not participate. Thus, Roger Finke and Christopher Scheitle ("Accounting for the Uncounted: Computing Correctives for the 2000 RCMS Data," *Review of Religious Research* 47, no. 1 [2005]) suggest that 62.7% is a more accurate national adherence rate than the 50% figure provided by the RCMS. Further, the uncounted adherents vary by county, state, and region, often reflecting the racial makeup of the area. Areas with larger black populations (e.g., the South) tend to have deflated RCMS adherence rates. Thus, Finke and Scheitle calculated adjusted adherent statistics (available at http://rra.hartsem.edu/finkescheitlearticle.htm).

3. *Religious Congregations and Membership in the United States 2000* (Nashville: Glenmary Research Center) describes a comparable faith family as "Evangelical Protestant." The RCMS authors drew on several sources to classify denominations: an article coauthored by Brian Steensland, Jerry Park, Mark Regnerus, Lynn Robinson, Bradford Wilcox, and Robert Woodberry, "The Measure of American Religion: Toward Improving the State of the Art," *Social Forces* 79 (2000): 291–318; J. Gordon Melton's *Encyclopedia of American Religions,* 6th ed. (Detroit: Gale Group, 1998); and Frank S. Mead, Samuel S. Hill, and Craig D. Atwood's *Handbook of Denominations in the United States,* 12th ed. (Nashville: Abingdon Press, 2005).

4. Data from *Religious Congregations and Membership in the United States 2000*; analyses by Dale Jones, Church Growth Research Center, Church of the Nazarene (e-mail message to authors, June 13, 2006).

5. Cynthia Woolever and Deborah Bruce, *Beyond the Ordinary: Ten Strengths of U.S. Congregations* (Louisville, KY: Westminster John Knox Press, 2004).

6. "Red state vs. blue state divide," from Wikipedia (http://en.wikipedia.org/wiki/Red_states).

7. From Michael Moncur's Collection of Quotations (http://www.quotationspage.com).

Chapter Two: Strength in Religious Geography

1. Robert Benchley's Law of Distinction, Robert Benchley, *The Best of Robert Benchley* (New York: Wings, 1996).

2. Gary Farley, Pickens Baptist Institute; quotes appeared in "Small Church Ministry Breakfast: Farley Delights with Harmonica, Inspires with Hope for Rural Churches," by Erin S. Cox-Holmes, Presbyterian News Service (http://www.pcusa.org/ga217/newsandphotos/ga06125.htm), June 21, 2006.

3. Gary Farley credits church consultant Lyle Schaller for the "Made in America" description.

4. *Baltimore Evening Sun,* July 15, 1925 (quoted in http://en.wikipedia.org/wiki/Bible_Belt).

5. See the Religion by Region Series, copublished by the Leonard E. Greenberg Center for the Study of Religion in Public Life at Trinity College and AltaMira Press. The states included here (with the exception of Kansas) correspond to two regions identified in that series, specifically C. R. Wilson and M. Silk, eds., *Religion and Public Life in the South: In the Evangelical Mode* (Walnut Creek, CA: AltaMira Press, 2005), and W. Lindsey and M. Silk, eds., *Religion and Public Life in the Southern Crossroads: Showdown States* (Walnut Creek, CA: AltaMira Press, 2004).

6. The sixteen states are Alabama, Arkansas, Florida, Georgia, Kansas, Kentucky, Louisiana, Mississippi, Missouri, North Carolina, Oklahoma, South Carolina, Tennessee, Texas, Virginia, and West Virginia.

7. C. Dwight Dorough, *The Bible Belt Mystique* (Philadelphia: Westminster Press, 1974), 196–202.

8. *Religious Congregations and Membership in the United States 2000* (Nashville: Glenmary Research Center).

9. See the work of Daniel V. A. Olson, Purdue University, whose research focuses on how religious pluralism at the county level affects church attendance and participation. For example, Daniel Olson, David Voas, and Alasdair Crockett, "Religious Pluralism and Participation: Why Previous Research Is Wrong," *American Sociological Review* 67 (2002): 212–30.

10. Karel Dobbelaere, "Secularization," in *Encyclopedia of Religion and Social Science*, ed. William H. Swatos (Walnut Creek, CA: AltaMira Press, 1998).

11. Bob Greene, *Once upon a Town: The Miracle of the North Platte Canteen* (New York: HarperCollins, 2002).

12. The county is 66% "churched." Data from *Religious Congregations and Membership in the United States 2000*. The "Adjusted Totals" include all adherents in the denominations counted by the Association of Statisticians of American Religious Bodies (ASARB) and estimate adherent totals for the historically African American denominations and other religious groups not listed in the ASARB totals. Roger Finke and Christopher P. Scheitle review how these estimates were computed ("Accounting for the Uncounted," *Review of Religious Research* 47, no. 1 [2005]).

Chapter Three: Strength in the Community

1. A three-mile radius represents a compromise between the best geography for rural areas (where a five-mile radius might be most appropriate) and the best geography for population-dense, urban areas (where a one-mile radius might work well).

2. A two-step cluster procedure was used to identify these community types. Cluster analysis groups cases or objects (in this case, congregations and their associated communities) into similar categories (in this case, community types) so that the association of objects is maximized if they are in the same group and minimized if they are in different groups.

3. Remember that any single congregation can score higher or lower than what is average for congregations in similar areas.

4. Cynthia Woolever and Deborah Bruce, *Beyond the Ordinary: Ten Strengths of U.S. Congregations* (Louisville, KY: Westminster John Knox Press, 2004).

5. Small congregations with fewer than 100 in worship are more common in Rural communities. Mid-size (100 to 350 in worship) and large congregations (more than 350 in worship) are somewhat more common in Growing Suburbs and Small Cities/Stable Suburbs. The distribution of congregations by size in Economically Distressed Urban areas and High-Mobility Urban communities matches the overall distribution of congregations.

6. Shawn McMullen and Mary Elizabeth Hopkins, "Common Size, Uncommon Impact," *Outreach Magazine*, July/August 2006 (http://www.outreachmagazine.org).

Chapter Four: Strength in a Perfect Match

1. Richard M. Burton and Borge Obel, *Strategic Organizational Diagnosis and Design: The Dynamics of Fit*, 3rd ed. (Boston: Kluwer Academic Publishers, 2004).

2. First documented by H. Paul Douglas, *The Church in the Changing City* (New York: Doran, 1927).

3. Burton and Obel, *Strategic Organizational Diagnosis and Design*.

4. We developed six measures for capturing the congregation-community match. After extensive statistical analyses, we determined that the absolute value difference between the community and congregation percentages was the appropriate measure. This measurement told us the most about the match dynamic and congregational vitality.

5. The findings for Catholic parishes and mainline Protestant churches should be considered with less certainty. In both faith groups, very few congregations matched their community on the 18-to-44 age-group trait (only fourteen Catholic parishes and ten mainline Protestant churches). These small numbers make statistical tests for significance less meaningful. However, we believe additional cases in the sample would yield a similar pattern of results.

6. James W. Lewis, "American Denominational Studies: A Critical Assessment," from Resources for American Christianity, http://www.resourcingchristianity.org.

Chapter Five: Multiple Sources of Geographic Strength

1. Cynthia Woolever and Deborah Bruce, *Beyond the Ordinary: Ten Strengths of U.S. Congregations* (Louisville, KY: Westminster John Knox Press, 2004).

2. Some church consultants believe congregations that moved or began after 1960 are more likely to grow numerically (see Lyle E. Schaller, *A Mainline Turnaround: Strategies for Congregations and Denominations* [Nashville: Abingdon Press, 2005]). Our data do not support this claim, but we have a limited number of Protestant cases that fit this criterion. Multiple factors produce numerical growth, not just relocation. Congregations willing to relocate probably have other strengths as well. They are willing to take risks and make changes. Congregations that are unwilling to change are not likely to be effective by going or by staying.

3. As quoted in "Under the Radar," *NetResults*, May/June 2004, 12–13.

4. Jason Byassee, "Emerging Model: A Visit to Jacob's Well," *Christian Century*, September 19, 2006, 20–24.

5. Stephen Hawking (with Leonard Mlodinow) recounts this story in *A Briefer History of Time* (New York: Bantam Dell Publishing Group, 2005), 1. The scientist in the conversation is said to be Bertrand Russell.

Conclusion

1. Adapted from Walter Brueggemann, "Counterscript: Living with the Elusive God," *Christian Century*, November 29, 2005, 22–28. We assume responsibility for any distortions in our application of Brueggemann's concepts.

2. Ibid., p. 22.

3. Many thanks to Beverly Prestwood-Taylor and Karen Nell Smith, cofounders of the

Brookfield Institute (http://www.brookfieldinstitute.org), for allowing us to use this distinction they developed for their "Walking in the Way of Peace" program.

4. Brueggemann, "Counterscript," 24.

Appendix 3

1. Cynthia Woolever and Deborah Bruce, *A Field Guide to U.S. Congregations: Who's Going Where and Why* (Louisville, KY: Westminster John Knox Press, 2002).

2. Cynthia Woolever and Deborah Bruce, *Beyond the Ordinary: Ten Strengths of U.S. Congregations* (Louisville, KY: Westminster John Knox Press, 2004).